spectacular
cakes

mich turner
spectacular cakes

photography Janine Hosegood

jacqui
small

I dedicate this book to the boys in my life –
my husband Phil, my son Marlow and in
memory of William. Together you are my
eternal inspiration.

First published in 2005 by
Jacqui Small LLP,
an imprint of Aurum Press Ltd,
7 Greenland Street, London NW1 0ND

Text copyright © Mich Turner
Photography, design and layout copyright
© Jacqui Small 2005

The right of Mich Turner to be identified as
the Author of this Work has been asserted
by her in accordance with the Copyright
Designs and Patent Act 1988.

Publisher Jacqui Small
Editorial Manager Kate John
Editor Anne McDowall
Designers Maggie Town and Beverly Price
Production Peter Colley

A catalogue record for this book is
available from the British Library.

ISBN 978 1 903221 39 6

2011

10 9 8 7 6

Printed and bound in Singapore

contents

introduction

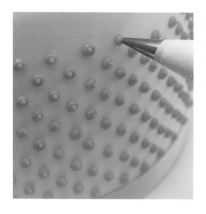

Welcome to my first book on spectacular cakes. The designs included here can be adapted to create perfect cakes for a variety of special occasions, including weddings, anniversaries, birthdays, christenings and bar mitzvahs. Whether you are a novice or a more experienced cake decorator, I hope you will be encouraged to recreate these designs using the detailed instructions and photographs as well as inspired to design your own spectacular cakes.

There are several things to bear in mind when choosing or designing a special-occasion cake. Firstly, what is the event? Who is the cake for and what would be their preference? Will the cake be traditional or contemporary in design? Should it be something formal or more fun and funky? Does the occasion call for a tiered, perfectly iced cake or would a sculptural chocolate creation studded with chocolate-dipped fruit be a better option? You should also take into consideration the venue: marquees can be particular hazards for multi-tiered cakes – opt instead for a stacked cake or perhaps a chocolate

helter-skelter; time of year – a light summer pavlova or a rich chocolate truffle torte?; number of guests and the mood of the occasion – create a cake with drama for a large social gathering or use individual cakes presented on a tiered stand for a more intimate setting. Consider, too, the colours, flowers and particular themes that have been chosen for the event.

In addition to the above, you'll need to decide on the flavour of the cake (see cake recipes, pages 12–19), its size and shape, and how to stack or support a tiered cake (see pages 34–7). But the most important thing is to enjoy your cake decorating! It can be immensely comforting to bake cakes and cookies to share, and even more satisfying to decorate a special cake – and it often means so much more to the recipient to know how much time, love and attention you have devoted to it. I challenge you to have a go!

cake techniques

cake preparation

A truly spectacular cake starts with a well-baked cake. In this book you will find cakes baked in many shapes and sizes – round, square, oval, heart, hexagonal and petal shaped. It is well worth taking the time to line your tins properly and accurately to produce a cake with a good, even shape. The recipes included in this book are all tried and tested at Little Venice Cake Company for our range of special wedding and celebration cakes. A special wedding cake is usually served after a substantial banquet. Cakes with intense flavours will stand up to a champagne toast, will reignite the taste buds, and your guests will not have to eat a huge slice for their palates to be satisfied.

Cakes should generally be covered two days and stacked the day before you wish to decorate them. Fix ribbon around the boards after cakes are decorated.

tiering cakes

Because the cake recipes that follow have a more dense texture than some other cakes, they are able to provide support when presented in tiers. Always position the more dense cakes at the base of a finished tiered cake, reserving the lighter cakes for higher up. A rich fruit cake will support the weight of the other tiers, adding stability.

In order of density, beginning with the lightest, the cakes are as follows:

Coffee and walnut cake (page 14)
Luscious lemon cake (page 15)
Chocolate truffle torte (page 13)
Moist carrot cake (pages 16–17)
Traditional rich fruit cake (pages 18–19)

While it is feasible to have a 5-tier cake constructed from 5 different flavours, I have found providing a choice of 2 flavours to be practical and sufficient.

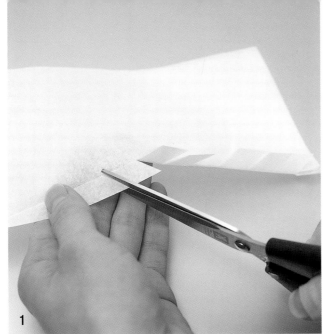

lining the tins

1 Take a piece of non-stick baking paper at least twice the size of the base of the tin and fold it in half. Place the tin over the folded paper and draw around the base in pencil. Cut out the 2 pieces just inside the pencil marks. Fold a sheet of baking paper long enough to line the circumference, or all sides, of the tin in half lengthways, making sure it reaches at least 2cm (¾in) above the top of the tin. From the folded crease, turn up 2cm (¾in) and press hard to form a sharp crease. Cut diagonal snips along the folded edge of the paper up to the crease.

2 Brush the inside base and sides of the tin with sunflower or groundnut oil. Place a paper disk in the base of the tin. Gently ease the strip of baking paper inside the tin as shown, pushing the diagonal snips into the edges and corners. Brush around the snips with sunflower oil and place the final disk of baking paper on top. (Line a square or other shaped tin in a similar way, making sure that the corners fit neatly.)

you will need

cake tin

non-stick baking paper

pencil

scissors

sunflower or groundnut oil

pastry brush

Tip When baking the rich fruit cake, fold a piece of brown paper in half and tie it around the outside of the tin with string. This prevents the sides of the cake becoming overcooked.

cake recipes

These cake recipes all have an intense flavour with a rather more dense texture than a standard cake. The chocolate, lemon and coffee and walnut cakes work particularly well, whether they are covered in marzipan and icing or lathered with smooth glossy chocolate and served for pudding.

chocolate truffle torte

This chocolate truffle cake is made with melted chocolate and its texture is similar to a chocolate brownie. It's delicious split and filled with chocolate ganache buttercream (see page 23), which gives it extra flavour. You can then cover it with marzipan and icing and hand decorate it or, for a decadent pudding, cover it with chocolate ganache and serve with fresh berries.

There is comparatively little flour in this recipe, which relies on the chocolate and eggs for support. The cake is baked in two halves; this ensures that it cooks evenly while retaining an overall height of 9–10cm (3½–4in). As an alternative to a large cake, make individual cakes of 5cm (2in) diameter by stamping them out of a single layer.

ingredients	6in round/square	8in round/square	10in round/square	12in round/square
plain chocolate (70% cocoa solids), broken into pieces	200g (7oz)	400g (14oz)	600g (1lb 5oz)	800g (1lb 12oz)
unsalted butter, softened	250g (9oz)	500g (1lb 2oz)	750g (1lb 10oz)	1kg (2lb 4oz)
light brown sugar	350g (12oz)	700g (1lb 8oz)	1.05kg (2lb 5oz)	1.4kg (3lb)
medium eggs, beaten	5	10	15	20
vanilla extract	1½tsp	1tbsp	1½tbsp	2tbsp
plain flour, sieved	140g (5oz)	275g (10oz)	410g (14½oz)	560g (1lb 4oz)
bake fan 140°C (275°F) conventional 160°C (325°F) gas 3	45min	1hr	1hr 20min	1hr 40min

1 Preheat the oven. Melt chocolate carefully in a microwave or in a bowl over simmering water, then allow to cool. Have all the ingredients at room temperature. Grease and line 2 sandwich cake tins. Beat together butter and sugar until light and fluffy. Add beaten egg, a little at a time, beating between each addition.

2 Pour the cooled melted chocolate slowly into the creamed mixture, beating all the time. Stir in the vanilla extract, then fold in the sieved flour.

3 Spoon mixture evenly into tins and bake for the time stated. The baked cakes should be well risen with a crust but should still wobble when shaken gently. Remove cakes from oven and allow to cool before turning out onto a wire rack. The crust will sink back onto the cake.

To store This cake will keep for up to 10 days once covered and decorated or wrapped in greaseproof paper and kept in an airtight container. If you refrigerate it, allow time for the cake to come up to room temperature before eating it. It is also suitable for freezing – allow to defrost overnight.

To serve When you are ready to decorate the cake, you can simply sandwich the 2 halves together with chocolate ganache buttercream. For greater luxury, slice each cake horizontally in half and sandwich with a further layer of buttercream. (This is only advisable if you are able to serve the cake with a plate and fork.) For individual cakes of 5cm (2in) diameter, split one cake horizontally and sandwich halves together with chocolate ganache buttercream.

coffee and walnut cake

This coffee and walnut cake is wonderfully sophisticated. Part of the reason for its delicious appeal is the use of the best-quality ingredients – Californian walnuts and real espresso coffee. Don't be tempted to substitute instant coffee granules here: the cake will taste much better – and be more indulgent – if you include a cup of real espresso. The coffee and walnut flavours are enhanced when the cake is layered with coffee buttercream and covered in glossy dark chocolate ganache for a true mocha experience. This is also a simple cake to make, thanks to its all-in-one method.

ingredients	6in round/square	8in round/square	10in round/square	12in round/square
unsalted butter, softened	175g (6oz)	325g (11½oz)	500g (1lb 2oz)	650g (1lb 7oz)
golden caster sugar	175g (6oz)	325g (11½oz)	500g (1lb 2oz)	650g (1lb 7oz)
medium eggs, beaten	3	6	9	12
self-raising flour, sieved	175g (6oz)	325g (11½oz)	500g (1lb 2oz)	650g (1lb 7oz)
baking powder, sieved	1½tsp	3tsp	5tsp	6tsp
ground coffee	2tbsp	4tbsp	6tbsp	12tbsp
boiling water	150ml (5fl oz) (to yield 3tbsp espresso)	225ml (8fl oz) (to yield 4–5tbsp espresso)	350ml (12fl oz) (to yield 5–6tbsp espresso)	450ml (16fl oz) (to yield 6–8tbsp espresso)
Californian walnuts, chopped	75g (2½oz)	150g (5½oz)	225g (8oz)	300g (10½oz)
vanilla extract	1tsp	2tsp	3tsp	4tsp
bake fan 160°C (325°F) conventional 180°C (350°F) gas 4	30min	45min	1hr	1hr 15min

1 Preheat the oven. Have all the ingredients at room temperature. Prepare 2 sandwich cake tins – grease and line with non-stick baking paper. Beat the softened butter for 1 minute in a large bowl with an electric whisk until light and fluffy. In a coffee plunger, pour the boiling water over the ground coffee and allow to infuse for 2 minutes. Plunge and pour the concentrated espresso into a small jug.

2 Add the sugar, eggs, sieved flour and baking powder, espresso and vanilla extract to the butter in the bowl and mix together for 5 minutes until light and fluffy. Fold in the chopped walnuts. The mixture should drop easily from a spoon.

3 Divide the mixture between the 2 prepared tins and bake for the time stated until risen and light golden in colour. A skewer inserted into the centre of the baked cake should come out clean.

To store This cake is best served and eaten fresh but will keep up to 4 days once covered and decorated or wrapped in greaseproof paper and kept in an airtight container. If frozen, allow to defrost overnight.

To serve When you are ready to decorate this cake, simply sandwich the halves together with espresso buttercream.

luscious lemon cake

This lemon cake recipe is light and refreshing, which makes it a lovely addition to any summer event and perfect for serving after a rich banquet as it refreshes the palate. It is also versatile: you can slice the cake horizontally in half and sandwich the halves together with lemon curd buttercream, then cover it either with marzipan and icing or with smooth chocolate ganache for a delectable pudding. As with the other cake recipes, it's important not to skimp on quality of ingredients. Although there are a lot of fresh lemons to zest and squeeze, the finished cake is well worth the effort!

ingredients	6in round/square	8in round/square	10in round/square	12in round/square
self-raising flour	140g (5oz)	275g (10oz)	500g (1lb 2oz)	800g (1lb 12oz)
plain flour	140g (5oz)	275g (10oz)	500g (1lb 2oz)	800g (1lb 12oz)
unsalted butter, softened	200g (7oz)	400g (14oz)	750g (1lb 10oz)	1.15kg (2lb 8oz)
golden caster sugar	200g (7oz)	400g (14oz)	750g (1lb 10oz)	1.15kg (2lb 8oz)
medium eggs, beaten	4	8	15	22
zest of fresh lemons	2	5	9	14
fresh lemon juice	2tbsp	75ml (2½fl oz)	125ml (4½fl oz)	200ml (7fl oz)
vanilla extract	2tsp	1tbsp	1½tbsp	2tbsp
for the syrup glaze: remainder of lemon juice	approx 100ml (3½fl oz)	approx 225ml (8fl oz)	approx 350ml (12fl oz)	approx 450ml (16fl oz)
golden caster sugar	85g (3oz)	140g (5oz)	225g (8oz)	300g (10½oz)
bake fan 140°C (275°F) conventional 160°C (325°F) gas 3	1hr 25min	1hr 40min	1hr 50min	2hr 10min

1 Preheat the oven. Have all the ingredients at room temperature. Grease and line the cake tin. Sieve flours together. Beat together butter and sugar until light and fluffy. Beat in eggs a little at a time, beating well between each addition. Add a few tablespoons of flour to prevent mixture from curdling. Carefully fold remaining flour into the creamed mixture. Stir in lemon zest, juice and vanilla extract. Spoon the mixture into the prepared tin and bake for the time stated until risen and light golden in colour. A skewer inserted into the centre of the baked cake should come out clean.

2 While the cake is baking, make the syrup glaze. Sieve the lemon juice into a small pan, add sugar, stirring all the time, and heat gently until sugar dissolves. Remove from heat. Once the cake is baked, remove from the oven and pierce with a skewer several times. Spoon over lemon syrup then leave cake to cool before removing it from the tin.

To store This cake is best served and eaten fresh but will keep up to 5 days once covered and decorated or wrapped in greaseproof paper and stored in an airtight container. If freezing, allow to defrost overnight.

moist carrot cake

This carrot cake – baked with walnuts, rum-soaked sultanas and coconut – makes a lovely, lighter alternative to a rich fruit cake. Once the cake is baked, it is spiked with a fresh citrus syrup, which helps keep it moist and fruity. So, too, does the use of sunflower oil, and because the recipe uses no dairy products, it is suitable for guests with a dairy intolerance. I used this recipe for the wedding cake I designed and made for Pierce Brosnan and Keely Shaye Smith and – at their request – I added chopped glacé ginger. Although no filling is necessary for this moist cake, it does taste particularly good if split and layered with fresh orange buttercream (see page 23).

ingredients	6in round/square	8in round/square	10in round/square	12in round/square
dark rum	25ml (1fl oz)	55ml (2fl oz)	75ml (2½fl oz)	100ml (3½fl oz)
sultanas	100g (3½oz)	200g (7oz)	300g (10½oz)	400g (14oz)
plain flour	175g (6oz)	350g (12oz)	525g (1lb 2½oz)	750g (1lb 10oz)
ground cinnamon	2tsp	4tsp	6tsp	8tsp
ground nutmeg	1tsp	2tsp	3tsp	4tsp
bicarbonate of soda	1tsp	2tsp	3tsp	4tsp
sunflower oil	150ml (5fl oz)	300ml (10fl oz)	450ml (16fl oz)	600ml (20fl oz)
golden caster sugar	75g (2½oz)	150g (5½oz)	225g (8oz)	300g (10½oz)
light brown sugar	75g (2½oz)	150g (5½oz)	225g (8oz)	300g (10½oz)
medium eggs, beaten	2	4	6	8
zest of fresh lemons	1	2	3	4
zest of fresh oranges	1	2	3	4
carrots, peeled and grated	175g (6oz)	350g (12oz)	525g (1lb 2½oz)	700g (1lb 8oz)
desiccated coconut	55g (2oz)	100g (3½oz)	150g (5½oz)	200g (7oz)
walnuts, chopped	55g (2oz)	100g (3½oz)	150g (5½oz)	200g (7oz)
vanilla extract	1tsp	2tsp	3tsp	4tsp
chopped glacé ginger (optional)	2tsp	1tbsp	1½tbsp	2tbsp
for the citrus syrup:				
light brown sugar	75g (2½oz)	115g (4oz)	150g (5½oz)	225g (8oz)
juice of fresh lemons	1	1½	2	3
juice of fresh oranges	1	1½	2	3
bake fan 140°C (275°F)				
conventional 150°C (300°F) gas 2	1hr 30min	2hr	2hr 30min	3hr

Tip When lining the tin, ensure the baking paper is at least 2cm (½in) above the height of the tin. Once the cake is skewered and the citrus syrup is poured over, it will appear flooded. This is perfectly normal and all this delicious juice will be absorbed into the cake.

1 Pour the rum over the sultanas and leave to infuse for 1 hour. Preheat the oven. Have all the ingredients at room temperature. Prepare the cake tin – grease and line with non-stick baking paper. Sieve the flour together with the ground cinnamon, ground nutmeg and bicarbonate of soda. Beat together the sunflower oil, sugar and eggs until smooth.

2 Stir the flour mixture into the smooth batter. Add the lemon and orange zest, grated carrot, desiccated coconut, walnuts, vanilla extract, chopped glacé ginger (if using) and marinated sultanas with all the risidual rum. Stir all the ingredients well to combine. Spoon the mixture into the prepared tin and bake for the time stated or until a skewer inserted into the centre of the cake comes out clean.

3 While the cake is baking, make the syrup. Place the sugar in a jug, then add the sieved lemon and orange juice. Stir well and continue to stir at intervals. Once the cake is baked, remove it from the oven and immediately pierce it with a skewer several times. Carefully spoon or pour over the citrus syrup then leave the cake to cool before removing it from the tin.

To store This cake keeps fresh for up to 14 days if covered and decorated with icing or wrapped in greaseproof paper and kept in an airtight container. Suitable for freezing. Allow to defrost overnight.

traditional rich fruit cake

I think it is essential to start with a really good, moist fruit cake for a celebration cake. In my recipe I have included dried dates, prunes and apricots alongside the more commonly used currants, raisins and sultanas: the flavour is more pronounced and a little less sweet. The molasses adds a rich treacle flavour.

This cake improves with keeping: ideally the baked cake should be matured for eight weeks before the event to improve the flavours, and it will keep for up to nine months once decorated with marzipan and icing if stored in a cool, dry place. If, following tradition, you want to reserve the top rich fruit tier of a wedding cake to serve at the first child's christening, wrap the decorated cake in a double layer of greaseproof paper followed by a double layer of aluminium foil. You can then store it in the freezer until required. The top tier of my wedding cake was frozen for six years before it was defrosted and served at my son Marlow's christening. Although this recipe is traditional for a wedding cake, it makes an equally good wedding anniversary, christening or Christmas cake.

ingredients	6in round/square	8in round/square	10in round/square	12in round/square
seedless currants	125g (4½oz)	250g (9oz)	375g (13oz)	500g (1lb 2oz)
sultanas	100g (3½oz)	200g (7oz)	300g (10½oz)	400g (14oz)
Californian raisins	100g (3½oz)	200g (7oz)	300g (10½oz)	400g (14oz)
whole pitted prunes, chopped	40g (1½oz)	75g (2½oz)	115g (4oz)	150g (5½oz)
whole dried apricots, chopped	40g (1½oz)	75g (2½oz)	115g (4oz)	150g (5½oz)
whole pitted dates, chopped	40g (1½oz)	75g (2½oz)	115g (4oz)	150g (5½oz)
natural-colour glacé cherries, chopped	50g (2oz)	100g (3½oz)	150g (5oz)	200g (7oz)
brandy (40% alcohol)	75ml (2½fl oz)	150ml (5½fl oz)	225ml (8fl oz)	300ml (10fl oz)
fresh lemons (juice and zest)	1	2	3	4
fresh oranges (juice and zest)	1	2	3	4
plain flour	175g (6oz)	350g (12oz)	525g (1lb 2½oz)	750g (1lb 10oz)
ground ginger	1tsp	2tsp	3tsp	4tsp
ground cinnamon	2tsp	4tsp	2tbsp	2½tbsp
ground nutmeg	1½tsp	1tbsp	1½tbsp	2tbsp
unsalted butter, softened	125g (4½oz)	250g (9oz)	375g (13oz)	500g (1lb 2oz)
light brown sugar	125g (4½oz)	250g (9oz)	375g (13oz)	500g (1lb 2oz)
medium eggs, beaten	2	4	6	8
molasses	½tbsp	1tbsp	1½tbsp	2tbsp
chopped almonds	25g (1oz)	55g (2oz)	75g (3oz)	115g (4oz)
bake fan 120°C (250°F) conventional 140°C (275°F) gas 2	3hr 30min	4hr	5hr	5½hr

1 Combine the currants, sultanas, raisins, prunes, apricots, dates and glacé cherries with the brandy and the fresh orange and lemon zest and juice. Leave to absorb for a minimum of 24 hours – ideally 72 hours.

2 Preheat the oven. Have all the ingredients at room temperature. Prepare the cake tin – grease and line with non-stick baking paper. Sieve the flour together with the ground ginger, cinnamon and nutmeg. Beat together the softened butter and sugar until light and fluffy. Beat in the eggs a little at a time, beating well between each addition. Add a few tablespoons of flour to prevent mixture from curdling.

3 Carefully fold the remaining flour into the creamed mixture. Stir in the molasses, then the soaked fruit (reserving the brandy in which it has been soaked) and the chopped nuts.

4 Spoon the mixture into the prepared tin and bake for the time stated. If the top of the cake appears to be browning too quickly, fold a sheet of greaseproof paper in half, cut a small hole the size of a walnut in the centre and carefully place it over the top of the cake. (Make sure you wear oven gloves to do so!)

5 When the cake is cooked, a skewer inserted into the centre should come out clean. Leave the cake until it is cold before removing it from the tin. Brush the top with the reserved brandy, then wrap the cake in a double layer of greaseproof paper and a double layer of aluminium foil to store.

Tip Buy ready-to-eat whole pitted dates, prunes and apricots and snip each piece into 3 using sharp kitchen scissors. This locks the moisture into the fruit. Ready-chopped fruit tends to dry out.

meringue

Meringues are very simple to make and require few ingredients. Because they do not contain any butter or oil, they are a healthier option than a rich cake. They are light and airy and less filling than a more traditional cake, which makes them perfect for a light summer party or canapé reception or after a rich wedding menu. Toasted chopped hazelnuts can be added to the mixture for extra flavour and texture.

ingredients	10 individual or one 8in	20 individual	30 individual	40 individual
medium egg whites	2	4	6	8
white caster sugar	115g (4oz)	225g (8oz)	350g (12oz)	450g (1lb)
vanilla extract	½tsp	½tsp	½tsp	1tsp
vinegar	½tsp	½tsp	½tsp	1tsp
finely chopped toasted hazelnuts (optional)	55g (2oz)	100g (3½oz)	150g (5½oz)	200g (7oz)

bake fan 120°C (250°F) conventional 150°C (300°F) gas 2:   30 minutes, then 4 hours

1 Preheat the oven. Have all the ingredients at room temperature. Place the egg whites in a clean, grease-free bowl and whisk on high speed until the egg white reaches the stiff peak stage. It should not be dry. Add the sugar 1 tablespoon at a time until the mixture is thick and glossy. Whisk in the vanilla extract and vinegar. If using hazelnuts, carefully fold them in at this stage.

2 For individual meringues, heap a dessertspoonful of the mixture onto a baking sheet lined with non-stick baking paper and hollow out the centre of each with the back of a metal dessertspoon. For 1 large meringue, draw a 20cm (8in) circle on the reverse of non-stick baking paper with a pencil. Use this as a guide for spreading the mixture. Hollow out the centre with the back of a metal spoon.

3 Place the meringues in the oven and immediately reduce the heat to 110°C (225°F) on a fan oven or 140°C (275°F/gas 1) on a conventional oven. After 30 minutes, turn the oven off and leave the meringues to dry out in the heat of the oven – ideally overnight but for at least 4 hours – until they are completely cold.

To serve When you are ready to serve the meringues, they can be lined with chocolate and, once set, filled with cream. Once filled, they should be eaten within 4 hours to prevent the meringue becoming soggy. Unfilled meringues can be stored in an airtight container until required for up to 4 weeks.

cookies

Hand-decorated cookies can be an effective way to extend the theme of a party. Personalise cookies for children by piping their names on them and present them in clear cellophane tied with a ribbon, or decorate them as butterflies with bright-coloured icing to make pretty table decorations.

spiced cookies

you will need

250g (9oz) self-raising flour

½ tsp ground cinnamon

½ tsp ground nutmeg

¼ tsp ground ginger

125g (4½oz) unsalted butter

125g (4½oz) light brown sugar

50g (2oz) ground almonds

½ tsp almond extract

1 large egg, beaten

to bake

fan 160°C (325°F)

conventional 180°C (350°F)

gas 4

10 minutes small cookies

14 minutes large cookies

Makes approximately 60 small cookies or 20 large cookies

1 Preheat the oven. Line a baking sheet with non-stick baking paper. Sieve flour, cinnamon, nutmeg and ginger into a bowl. Cut butter into small pieces and rub into the flour until the mixture resembles fine breadcrumbs. Stir in the sugar, ground almonds and almond extract. Stir in the beaten egg to bind the dough together and knead into a neat ball. Gather up the dough and wrap in cling film. Place in the refrigerator to rest for 20 minutes.

2 Roll out the dough on a lightly floured board to 5mm (¼in) thickness for small cookies or 1cm (½in) for large cookies. Place the cookies on the prepared baking sheet and bake in the oven until they are golden around the edges. Carefully lift the cookies onto a wire rack and allow them to cool completely before decorating them.

lemon and almond cookies

you will need

150g (5½oz) unsalted butter

150g (5½oz) golden caster sugar

1 medium egg, beaten

300g (10½oz) self-raising flour, sieved

zest of 2 fresh lemons

55g (2oz) ground almonds

½ tsp almond extract

to bake

fan 160°C (325°F)

conventional 180°C (350°F)

gas 4

8 minutes small cookies

12 minutes large cookies

Makes approximately 60 small or 20 large cookies

1 Preheat the oven. Have all the ingredients at room temperature. Line a baking sheet with non-stick baking paper. Beat together the softened butter and sugar until light and fluffy. Add half the beaten egg and whisk. Stir in the sieved flour, lemon zest, almonds, almond extract and the remainder of the egg to form a dough. Wrap in cling film and place in the refrigerator to rest for 20 minutes.

2 Roll out the dough onto a lightly floured board to 5mm (¼in) thickness for small cookies, 1cm (½in) for larger cookies. Place cookies on the lined baking sheet and bake in the oven until golden around the edges. Carefully lift the cookies onto a wire rack and allow them to cool before decorating them.

buttercream

Buttercream is a combination of softened unsalted butter and icing sugar. The basic mixture can be combined with other flavours: these lemon curd, espresso and chocolate ganache versions are particularly good.

you will need

250g (9oz) unsalted butter, softened

500g (1lb 2oz) icing sugar

1tsp vanilla extract

yields 750g (1lb 11oz)

Beat the softened butter for 2 minutes using an electric whisk. Sieve in the icing sugar and beat slowly at first. Add the vanilla extract then, with the whisk on full speed, whip until the buttercream is very light and fluffy.

lemon curd buttercream

The luscious lemon cake (see page 15) is so fresh and light it really needs little accompaniment, but a light, creamy lemon buttercream complements it beautifully. Simply stir 275g (10oz) of lemon curd into 1 quantity of buttercream..

espresso buttercream

The deliciously sophisticated coffee and walnut cake (see page 14) really benefits from the inclusion of a layer of espresso buttercream. Pour 150ml (5fl oz) freshly boiled water over 2 heaped tablespoons of ground coffee. Allow to infuse, then filter the liquid espresso. Add 2 tablespoons of cooled espresso – 3 for a more pronounced flavour – to 1 quantity of buttercream.

chocolate ganache buttercream

Chocolate ganache is a blend of boiled cream and chocolate. It has a smooth, rich, velvety texture that literally melts in the mouth. Mixed with buttercream it becomes a wonderfully decadent filling or frosting for the chocolate truffle torte (see page 13).

you will need

175g (6oz) dark chocolate (70% cocoa solids), broken into pieces

125g (4½oz) fresh double cream

1 quantity of buttercream

yields 1.05kg (2lb 5oz)

Place the chocolate pieces in a clean dry bowl. Bring the cream to the boil, remove from the heat and pour over the chocolate. Stir with a wooden spoon until the chocolate is melted and the ganache is smooth and glossy. Allow the chocolate ganache to cool for 15 minutes before beating it into the buttercream. Store any excess buttercream in the refrigerator for up to 2 weeks.

	6in	8in	10in	12in
to sandwich 2 halves	½ quantity	1 quantity	1½ quantity	2 quantity
to cover top and sides	½ quantity	1 quantity	1½ quantity	2 quantity

alternative flavours

Lime buttercream Add the zest of 1 lime and 3 drops of lime oil to 1 quantity of plain vanilla buttercream. This buttercream works well with the luscious lemon cake – particularly for individual ganache bites.

Orange buttercream Add the zest of 1 medium orange to 1 quantity of plain vanilla buttercream. This buttercream can be used to sandwich and cover layers of the moist carrot cake (see pages 16–7).

Toasted pecan buttercream Toast 55g (2oz) pecans under a grill, chop coarsely and add to 1 quantity of chocolate ganache buttercream. This is a particularly good option for cakes that are not being dressed with fresh fruit.

covering a cake with marzipan

One question I am asked more than any other is: 'Do I have to use marzipan?' We seem to be divided into lovers or loathers of this luxurious almond paste. I definitely fall into the first category – as a student I would bake my own fruit cakes with an additional layer of marzipan in the centre. In fact, apart from its taste, marzipan plays a threefold role as a covering for a fruit cake: firstly, it protects the baked cake, locking in moisture as the almonds have a rich oil content; secondly, it adds form and stability – especially if the cake is destined to become a tiered cake; thirdly, it provides a good clean base for the icing, which prevents the colour of the cake bleeding through. For multi-tiered cakes I recommend it as essential; however, you could cover a single-tier cake with a double layer of sugar paste instead if you wish.

for sugar paste

How you cover a cake with marzipan depends on whether you are going to be using sugar paste or royal icing. For sugar paste, the marzipan is rolled out and smoothed over the cake in one piece to create softly rounded edges.

you will need

cake

thin board the same size as the cake

pastry brush

boiled, sieved apricot jam

marzipan

icing sugar

rolling pin

smoother

turntable or bowl

sharp knife

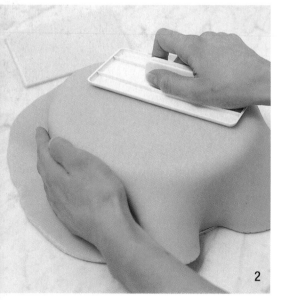

1 Place the cooled baked cake upside down on a thin cake board the same size as the cake and brush liberally with boiled, sieved apricot jam. Knead the marzipan until smooth and pliable. Dust the work surface lightly with icing sugar and roll the marzipan evenly into a size large enough to cover the top and sides of the cake, allowing for surplus (use string to measure). The marzipan should be approximately 5mm (¼in) thick. Carefully lift the marzipan onto the cake.

2 Smooth the top and sides of the cake using your hands and a smoother. Trim off the majority of the excess marzipan.

3 Lift the cake onto a turntable or upturned bowl and neatly trim the final excess marzipan using a sharp knife and keeping it flush with the bottom of the board.

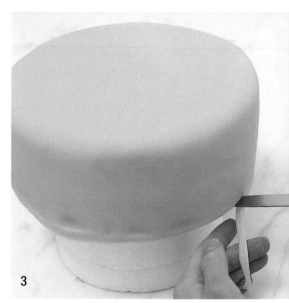

● round cake ■ square cake

size of cake	6in ●	6in ■	8in ●	8in ■	9in ●	9in ■	10in ●	10in ■	12in ●	12in ■	14in ●	14in ■	16in ●	16in ■
quantity	600g 1lb 5oz	750g 1lb 10oz	800g 1lb 12oz	1kg 2lb 4oz	1kg 2lb 4oz	1.25kg 2lb 12oz	1.25kg 2lb 12oz	1.5kg 3lb 8oz	1.75kg 3lb 8oz	2kg 4lb 8oz	2.25kg 5lb	2.65kg 5lb 13oz	2.85kg 6lb 4oz	3kg 6lb 10oz

for royal icing

Cakes covered with royal icing should have sharp, clean, angular edges and so the marzipan needs to be rolled out and applied as separate pieces. This method is more time consuming, but the finished result is well worth it.

you will need

cake
thick board 3in larger than the cake
pastry brush
boiled, sieved apricot jam
marzipan
icing sugar
rolling pin
sharp knife

Tip If the cake is very domed, slice the peak off to level the surface. You can roll a thin sausage of marzipan and use this to build up any uneven edges around the base of the cake once it has been turned upside down.

2

1 Place the cooled baked cake upside down in the centre of the baseboard and brush liberally with boiled, sieved apricot jam. Knead the marzipan until smooth and pliable. Dust the work surface lightly with icing sugar and roll the marzipan evenly into a size large enough to cut out the top and sides separately and accurately (use string or a ruler to measure). The marzipan should be approximately 5mm (¼in) thick.

2 Using both hands, carefully lift the marzipan onto the cake. Fix the top in position first, then apply each of the sides in turn. Trim any excess with a sharp knife. Allow to set overnight before applying the royal icing.

covering a cake with sugar paste

Sugar paste is a wonderful invention. Rolled out like marzipan and smoothed over the cake, this sweet paste creates a fast, clean, smooth finish with gently curved edges. It provides a very good base for additional decoration or looks clean, classical and contemporary simply adorned with fresh flowers. It is soft and pliable to apply; sets firm but not rock hard; cuts beautifully and has a shelf life of one year. However, It does not like to get wet – moisture will dissolve the sugar leaving craters, so keep all utensils clean and thoroughly dry.

you will need

marzipan-covered cake placed on a thin board of the same size

thick board 3in larger than the cake

pastry brush

icing sugar

sugar paste

rolling pin

smoother

sharp knife

brandy or cooled boiled water

turntable or bowl

palette knife

small quantity of royal icing

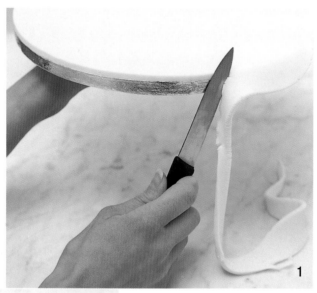

1 Brush the thick baseboard with cooled boiled water. Dust the work surface lightly with icing sugar (too much will dry the icing) and knead the sugar paste until smooth and pliable. Evenly roll the icing to the correct size – large enough to cover the baseboard and approximately 3mm (⅛in) thick. Carefully place the icing over the board and use a smoother to finish. Holding the board in one hand, use a sharp knife to cut away the excess, keeping the knife flush with the side of the board. Set aside to set (ideally overnight)

2 Brush the marzipan-covered cake with brandy or cooled boiled water. This acts as a good antiseptic seal between the marzipan and sugar paste as well as being an adhesive.

3 Dust the work surface lightly with icing sugar and knead the sugar paste until smooth and pliable. Evenly roll the sugar paste into a size large enough to cover the top and sides of the cake, allowing for surplus (use string to measure). It should be approximately 5mm (¼in) thick. Carefully lift the icing onto the marzipan-covered cake.

guide to quantities to cover cakes with sugar paste

● round cake ■ square cake

size of cake	6in ●	6in ■	8in ●	8in ■	9in ●	9in ■	10in ●	10in ■	12in ●	12in ■	14in ●	14in ■	16in ●	16in ■
quantity	750g 1lb 10oz	850g 1lb 14oz	1kg 2lb 4oz	1.25kg 2lb 12oz	1.25kg 2lb 12oz	1.5kg 3lb 8oz	1.5kg 3lb 8oz	1.8kg 4lb	2.1kg 4lb 10oz	2.35kg 5lb 3oz	2.7kg 6lb	3kg 6lb 10oz	3.25kg 7lb 3oz	3.5kg 7lb 11oz

guide to quantities to cover cake boards with sugar paste

size of cake	6in ●	6in ■	8in ●	8in ■	9in ●	9in ■	10in ●	10in ■	12in ●	12in ■	14in ●	14in ■	16in ●	16in ■
quantity	250g 9oz	350g 12oz	550g 1lb 3½oz	650g 1lb 7oz	700g 1lb 8oz	750g 1lb 10oz	800g 1lb 12oz	825g 1lb 13oz	825g 1lb 13oz	850g 1lb 14oz	900g 2lb	950g 2lb 2oz	950g 2lb 2oz	1kg 2lb 4oz

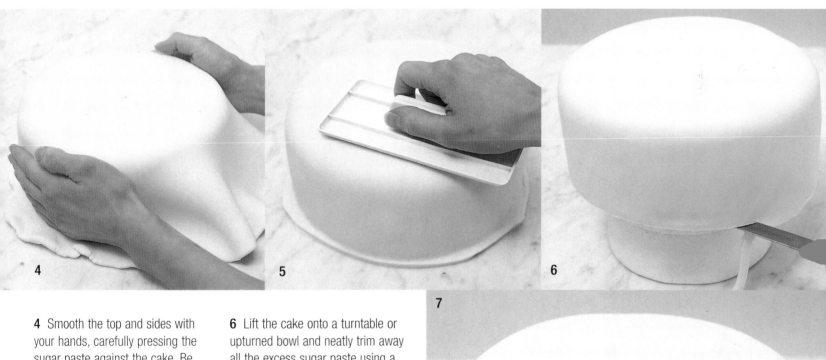

4   5   6

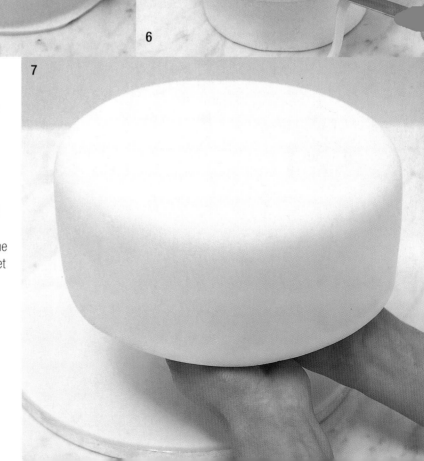

7

4 Smooth the top and sides with your hands, carefully pressing the sugar paste against the cake. Be careful not to drag the icing down the sides of the cake as this will cause it to crack and tear.

5 Use a smoother to give the cake a professional, clean finish and prick any air bubbles with a pin. Trim the majority of the excess sugar paste away from the cake.

6 Lift the cake onto a turntable or upturned bowl and neatly trim away all the excess sugar paste using a sharp knife, keeping the knife flush with the bottom of the board.

7 Slide a palette knife carefully underneath the cake and board and lift from underneath using both hands. Put a dab of royal icing on the pre-lined baseboard and carefully set the cake in position on top.

royal icing

Royal icing is traditional and is staging a comeback! Made from fresh egg white and icing sugar, royal icing is a sweet paste that is lathered onto the cake and allowed to set. Once made, royal icing will keep fresh in an airtight container for up to 7 days. It will separate if left for longer than 24 hours and should be rewhisked before using.

for piping:
1 medium egg white
350g (12oz) icing sugar, sieved
juice ½ lemon, sieved through a tea strainer
yields 400g (14oz)

Place the egg white into a clean, grease-free bowl and whisk until it forms very soft peaks. Add the icing sugar and whisk slowly at first until all the sugar is incorporated, then on full speed for 1 minute. Add the lemon juice and whisk for another minute.

for covering:
For icing to be used for covering a cake, add 1 teaspoon of glycerine per 450g (1lb) icing and omit the lemon juice. This will allow the icing to be cut without it splintering.

Tip Reconstituted albumen powder can be substituted for fresh egg white and is available from specialist cake suppliers. It should be used according to the manufacturer's instructions, but the ratio is generally 25g (1oz) albumen powder and 150ml (5fl oz) water to 900g (2lb) icing sugar.

guide to quantities to cover cakes with royal icing

● round cake ■ square cake

size of cake	6in ●	6in ■	8in ●	8in ■	9in ●	9in ■	10in ●	10in ■	12in ●	12in ■	14in ●	14in ■	16in ●	16in ■
quantity	800g 1lb 12oz	1kg 2lb 4oz	1kg 2lb 4oz	1.25kg 2lb 12oz	1.25kg 2lb 12oz	1.5kg 3lb 8oz	1.5kg 3lb 8oz	1.75kg 3lb 14oz	2kg 4lb 8oz	2.25kg 5lb	2.5kg 5lb 8oz	2.7kg 6lb	3kg 6lb 10oz	3.25kg 7lb 3oz

flooding icing

For flooding icing, thin the royal icing down with drops of egg white or water. Egg white will make the finished run-out stronger but the icing may take longer to dry. Thinning the icing with water will enable it to dry quicker but it will be less strong. Add additional liquid a drop at a time to the royal icing and stir gently. Do not beat the icing at this stage as you will incorporate too much air and bubbles will appear in the run-outs. To judge the amount of water to add, swirl a knife in the bowl and count steadily to 10 as the ripples subside.

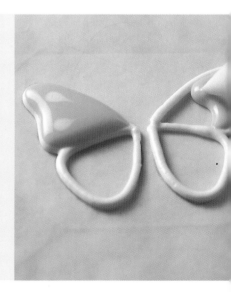

1

covering a cake with royal icing

Covering a cake with royal icing is a much more laborious technique than using sugar paste, as several coats are required to build the icing up to the desired thickness. It sets very firm and is somewhat brittle to slice, but the finished icing has a wonderfully sweet flavour and a clean, architectural finish that is perfect for particular designs, for example the 1950s chic and Art Deco cakes (see pages 118–9 and 134–5 respectively).

you will need

marzipan-covered cake placed on a thick baseboard 3in larger than the cake

fresh royal icing

palette knife

top and side scrapers

sharp knife

1 Prepare the royal icing. Use a palette knife to apply the royal icing liberally onto one of the sides of the marzipan-covered cake in a paddling motion to expel any air bubbles from the icing.

2 Hold a side scraper at a 45-degree angle to the cake and steadily and purposefully pull it towards you. Use a sharp knife in a downward motion to remove the excess icing from the 2 side ends and top edge. Repeat on the opposite side. Allow the icing to set for at least 8 hours before repeating the process on the other 2 sides.

2

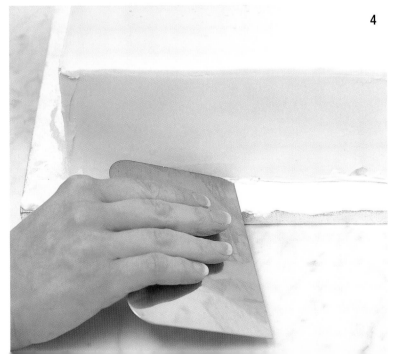

4

3 Spread the royal icing liberally on the top of the cake. Using a long scraper and holding the ends away from the cake, carefully pull the scraper at an angle of 45 degrees across the top of the cake towards you. Use a sharp knife to trim the edges. Allow to set for 8 hours in a warm, dry environment. Repeat steps 1–3 until all sides and the top of the cake have received 3 coats.

4 To cover the board, spread the royal icing onto each side in turn and, holding a side scraper at a 45-degree angle to the board, carefully pull it towards you. Clean the edges with a sharp knife.

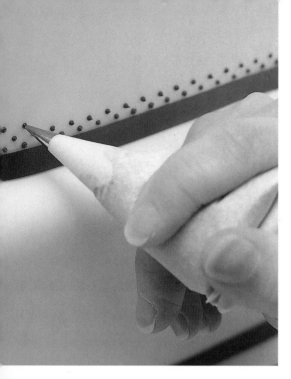

piping icing

All of the iced designs in this book are created using royal icing – a blend of egg white and icing sugar. The icing is whipped until it is glossy, at which point it will dry, harden and set on exposure to air. Royal icing can be prepared from fresh egg white (see page 28) or commercially produced dried albumen powder and is versatile in that it can be used for covering cakes, adding fine detail or can be thinned down for flooding run-outs. Once the royal icing is prepared, it is essential to keep it covered, either with a clean damp cloth or in an airtight container.

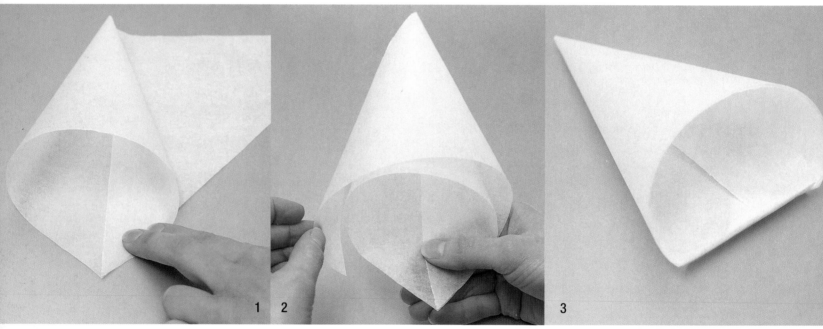

making a piping bag

Piping bags are made from triangles of non-stick baking paper. The larger the triangle, the larger the piping bag. I like to make various sizes – smaller ones for flooding lots of different colours and larger ones for piping single colours onto a number of tiers.

1 Fold a 30–45cm (12–18in) square of greaseproof paper in half diagonally to make 2 triangles and cut the paper in half along the crease. Place the paper on the table with the tip of the triangle facing you and bring the underside of the left point to the right of centre and hold with your thumb and forefinger.

2 Bring the right hand point up, over and round to the back to meet the centre.

3 Carefully fold the corner of the paper over to secure the bag, as shown.

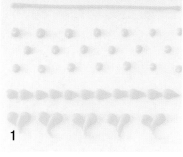
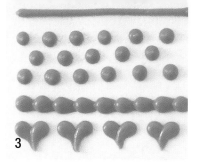
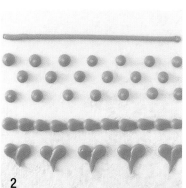

1

2

3

4

icing techniques

All the iced cakes in this book have been hand decorated using a piping bag filled with a nozzle and royal icing. Snip the end of the piping bag and drop in a nozzle. For flooding, the piping bag has no nozzle – the end is snipped once the bag is filled. Hold the bag and fill two-thirds full with royal icing. Fold the highest point of the bag over and tuck the sides in to prevent the icing oozing out. Hold the bag in your hand between your second and third fingers and use your thumb on the top of the bag to exert pressure to force the icing out in a controlled manner.

1 No. 1.5 nozzle – small plain nozzle
Used for small pearls, vanity fair, tiffany pearl ribbon and outlines for all run-outs.

2 No. 2 nozzle – medium plain nozzle
Used for brush embroidery, smaller pearls, Fabergé and fleur-de-lis designs.

3 No. 3 nozzle – large plain nozzle
Used for bead trails around the base of cakes and for candy stripe design.

4 No. 5 nozzle – star nozzle
Used for star trails around the base of the cakes, individual stars and scroll hearts.

glazing

There are a number of lustres and edible gels available, which can dramatically enhance elements of a hand-iced cake. Pearls can be brought to life with edible gel to maintain a dewy appearance and whole sections of icing can be brushed with lustres mixed with alcohol dipping solution for an authentic sparkle.

edible gel

Made from a sugar glucose solution, edible gel can be brushed neatly onto set icing to create an instant wet look. The gel remains slightly tacky even when set so be careful when handling the finished cake.

edible gel mixed with lustres

For the fleur-de-lis (see pages 126–7) and the Fabergé cake (see pages 130–1), shown here, I have mixed ½ teaspoon of topaz lustre with 1 teaspoon of edible gel to create a paste. This is then brushed onto the pearls for an authentic dewy pearly shine. Various colours of lustres are available including ruby, sapphire, jade, copper and gold.

lustres mixed with alcohol dipping solution

Lustres can also be dissolved in alcohol and brushed onto set icing as on vanity fair and caramel tiara cakes (see pages 132–3 and 138). The alcohol allows you to brush the lustre onto the pearls but then evaporates, leaving a matt-sheen appearance. Be careful, as the lustre will brush off or mark the cake if it is touched.

individual cake stands

Small cakes presented on a stand are becoming increasingly popular and are an effective way to create height and drama for more intimate celebrations. Here I have shown how to make two display stands: an iced one for individual iced cakes and a chocolate one to present chocolate cakes or pavlova. Stands can be made in many shapes and sizes – round, square and hexagonal are the most practical. Decide on the number and size of tiers and calculate the quantity of individual cakes you will need using the table below.

iced stand

The individual iced cakes shown in this book (see pages 49, 108–9 and 140–3) are presented on iced stands. I like to co-ordinate the colour of the icing on the stand and the ribbon with the mini cakes.

you will need

icing sugar
sugar paste
rolling pin
cake boards
pastry brush
smoother
glue stick
15mm (⅝in) width ribbon, sufficient length to edge boards and wrap around central columns
polystyrene colums
royal icing

Tip Make your top tier no smaller than 8in diameter. This will allow the tier below to have an acceptable size polystyrene column to support the top tier while providing sufficient space to display the cakes.

1 Lightly dust a work surface with icing sugar. Knead the sugar paste until pliable and smooth. Working on one board at a time, roll out paste large enough to cover the board to 5mm (¼in) thick.

2 Brush the board with cold water then lift the icing over the board. Smooth the icing then, holding the knife against the board, cut away the excess icing.

3 Rub glue stick around the edge of the board and attach a length of 15mm (⅝in) width ribbon. Rub glue over the polystyrene column and wrap the ribbon around it, starting at the bottom edge and working your way up, carefully overlapping as you go until you reach the top edge. Glue the final piece into position.

4 Fix the central columns into position with royal icing on each tier and allow to set overnight. Assemble the stand by securing the tiers together with royal icing.

size of board	round stand		square stand		hexagonal stand	
	5cm (2in) diam cakes/pavlova	4cm (1½in) ganache bites	5cm (2in) diam cakes/pavlova	4cm (1½in) ganache bites	5cm (2in) diam cakes/pavlova	4cm (1½in) ganache bites
8in	5	7	8	10	6	9
10in	9	12	12	15	8	11
12in	10	15	12	20	11	15
14in	12	18	16	24	12	18
16in	14	20	20	28	14	20
18in	17	24	24	30	16	24

chocolate-covered stand

Chocolate stands can be painted with white or dark chocolate: white chocolate creates the right look for a wedding cake, while dark chocolate stands are suitable for cocktail and dinner parties. Coating chocolate, though inappropriate for use in recipes, is ideal for covering cake stands: it is less expensive than real chocolate and sets very quickly once melted and painted onto the stand as it contains a high percentage of vegetable fat.

1

2

you will need

glue stick or royal icing

7.5cm- (3in-) high polystyrene columns

cake boards

coating chocolate

50mm (2in) paintbrush

edible spray varnish (optional)

1 Glue or ice the polystyrene columns onto the centre of each board, except the top one. Melt the coating chocolate in a bowl over simmering water or in a microwave. Using a 50mm (2in) paintbrush, paint the chocolate over the board and up the sides of the polystyrene.

2 Glue or ice the stand together ensuring each tier is centrally positioned. For added protection, spray the stand with an edible spray varnish. Store the stand in a cool, dry place out of direct sunlight or heat until required.

Tip Once the polystyrene columns are positioned, the stand should still have at least 7.5cm (3in) space all around to hold the cakes comfortably.

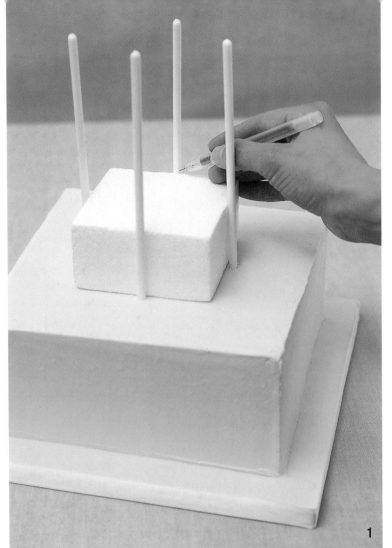

blocking a cake

Blocking a cake with fresh flowers or fruit is a stunning way to present it and creates an illusion that each tier is suspended on a bed of fruit or flowers. Blocking is also one of the most stable methods of stacking tiers. The polystyrene blocks provide surface-area stability for the tier above and also a base for wired flowers.

1 Place the polystyrene blocks in the centre of the 2 largest tiers. Insert a dowel at the centre point of each side of the block, making sure they are straight and pushed down to the boards. Mark each dowel where it meets the top of the block.

2 Remove dowels and line up on a table. Using a ruler and pen, re-mark each one to the highest point. (This will ensure the cake is level and supported when the dowels are reinserted and the next tier is stacked into position.) Cut each dowel to the new mark. Replace the dowels in each cake so they are flush with the top of the polystyrene blocks.

3 Using both hands, gently lift the middle tier, carefully positioning it on the block of the base one until it is central, stable and even. Repeat with the top tier. Edge each board with ribbon, securing it at the back of the cake with glue.

1

you will need

3 cake tiers, covered with marzipan and royal icing and placed centrally on thick boards 7.5cm (3in) larger than each cake, covered with royal icing

2 polystyrene blocks, 5cm (2in) deep and 10cm (4in) smaller than the medium-sized and largest cake tier

8 dowels

pen

ruler

sharp heavy-duty scissors or a junior hacksaw

15mm (⅝in) width ribbon to edge each board

glue stick

Tip Make sure that you scale the polystyrene blocks with the size of the tiers to maintain stability and to allow sufficient space for the flowers or fruit.

3

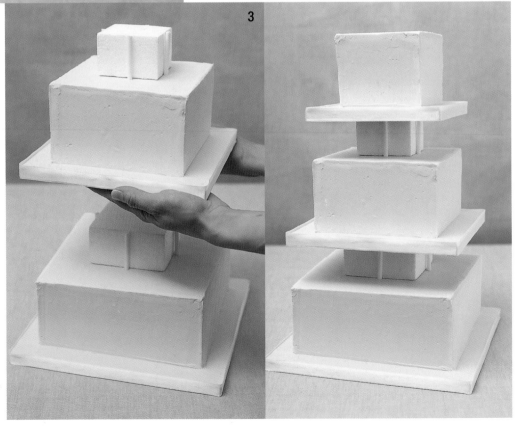

stacking a cake

Stacking is a preferred American way to present a finished wedding cake. The tiers, which are stacked either centrally over each other or offset, are supported with hidden boards and dowels. The overall height of a stacked cake is less than other tiered cakes. For a grander effect, you can increase the number of tiers, including some false upper tiers if necessary.

1 Spread a small amount of royal icing on the larger baseboard and fix the smaller board in position by pressing it firmly. Place a small amount of royal icing on the top baseboard and position the base cake tier centrally on top. Push 6 dowels randomly into the centre of the cake, making sure their line does not fall outside the size of the tier to be stacked above. Use a pen to mark each dowel at the point it surfaces from the cake.

2 Remove the dowels and line them up on a table. Find the average mark and, using a ruler and pen, mark each of the dowels at the same point. (This will ensure the cake is level and supported when the dowels are reinserted and the next tier is placed into position.) Cut each dowel to the new mark using heavy-duty scissors or a junior hacksaw. Check each dowel is the correct length before reinserting them all into the cake as they will be very difficult to remove again. Once the dowels are pushed right into the cake, spread a small amount of royal icing on the centre of the cake with a palette knife.

3 Use both hands to gently hold the next tier and carefully position it onto the base cake. Repeat step 2 with another 6 dowels before placing the top tier into position. Cut lengths of 25mm (1in) width ribbon to fix around each tier. Secure these in place with a dab of royal icing at the back and base of each tier. Edge each of the 2 iced baseboards with 15mm (⅝in) width ribbon, using glue stick to secure it in position. Ensure that the joins are at the back of the cakes.

Tip Leave the cakes for 24 hours after covering them with marzipan and icing before attempting to stack them. This allows time for the marzipan and icing to harden and set so that you will be able to handle the tiers without the icing cracking or dimpling.

you will need

3 cake tiers covered with marzipan and icing and placed on thin boards of the same size and shape

2 baseboards, 7.5cm (3in) and 15cm (6in) larger than base tier, covered with icing

royal icing

12 dowels

pen

ruler

sharp heavy-duty scissors or a junior hacksaw

palette knife

25mm (1in) width ribbon to fix around each tier

15mm (⅝in) width ribbon to edge baseboards

glue stick

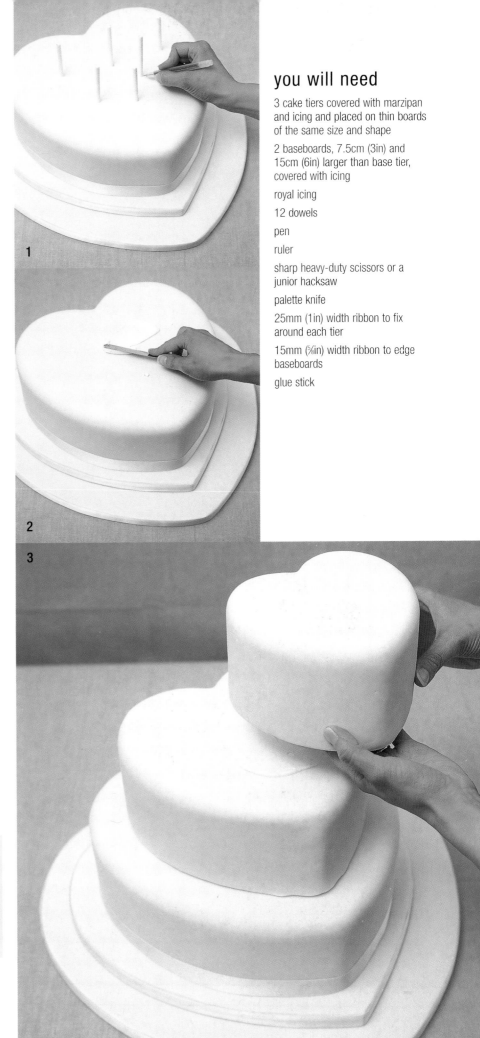

using pillars to separate tiers

Separating tiers with pillars is a traditional way to add dramatic height and grandeur to a cake and the space created between the tiers can be dressed with fresh, sugar or silk flowers. Pillars are available in many heights, colours and finishes – dowels placed inside the pillars carry all the weight of the tiers. With very large or heavy tiers, increase the number of pillars – the grid supplied (see page 146) has markings for 3, 4, 6 or 8 pillars on each tier.

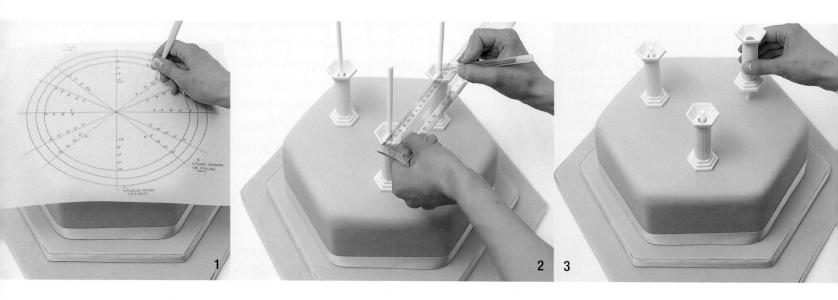

you will need

3 cake tiers, each covered with marzipan and sugar paste

4 thick boards, 7.5cm (3in) larger than each cake tier and one 15cm (6in) larger than the base tier, covered with sugar paste

grid template (see page 146)

scribe

6 dowels

6 x 9cm (3½in) pillars

ruler

pen

sharp heavy-duty scissors or a junior hacksaw

15mm (⅝in) width ribbon to edge each baseboard

glue stick

1 Start with all cakes positioned on boards and the base tier on the largest baseboard. Place the grid template centrally over the largest tier and use a scribe to mark 3 points along guide C.

2 Insert a dowel into each of the marked points and drop a pillar over the top. Place a ruler across 2 of the pillars and mark the dowels at the top of the pillars with a pen. Move the ruler around to between one of these pillars and the third one and finally between this pillar and the first one marking the rods each time. Remove the pillars and dowels from the cake.

3 Line the dowels up and use a ruler to measure and a pen to mark the average point. This will ensure the cake is level and supported when the dowels are replaced and the next tier is stacked into position. Cut each dowel to the new mark using heavy-duty scissors or a junior hacksaw. Replace the dowels into cake and position a pillar carefully over each one.

4 Repeat the above with the middle tier. Edge each of the iced baseboards with 15mm (⅝in) width ribbon and secure in position with glue stick, ensuring that the point at which the ribbon joins on each of the boards is facing the back of the cake. Finally, stack the tiers, making sure they are level, stable and centred.

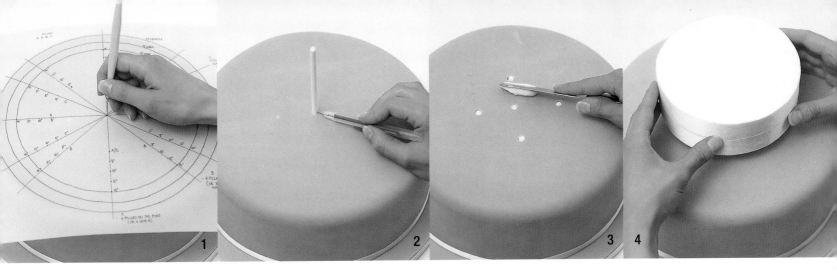

stacking tiers with a central column

Separating cake tiers with a central column gives a contemporary, uncluttered look and wrapping the column in a contrasting or complementary ribbon creates a dramatic or more subtle effect. It's not necessary to add finishing touches between the tiers so this technique is popular for designs that reach or cover the top of each tier so that they can be clearly seen.

you will need

3 cake tiers, covered with marzipan and sugar paste

3 baseboards, 7.5cm (3in) larger than each cake tier, covered with sugar paste

grid template (see page 146)

scribe

dowels

ruler and pen

sharp heavy-duty scissors or a junior hacksaw

2 polystyrene blocks, 5cm (2in) deep and 10cm (4in) smaller than the medium-sized and largest cake tier

25mm (1in) width ribbon to edge each polystyrene block

glue stick

2 thin boards of the same size and shape as the polystyrene blocks

royal icing

15mm (⅝in) width ribbon to edge each baseboard

Tip As this technique is less stable than other methods for tiering cakes, restrict its use to a maximum of 4 tiers.

1 Start with cakes positioned on boards. Place the grid template centrally over the largest cake and mark the centre point onto the cake with a scribe.

2 Insert one dowel into the centre of the largest cake, making sure it is straight and pushed down to the cake board. Mark the dowel with a pen at the point where it surfaces from the top of the cake. Remove the dowel and line it up with 4 others. Use a ruler and pen to mark each dowel to the measured point. (This will ensure that the cake is level and supported when the dowels are replaced and the next tier is stacked into position.)

3 Cut each dowel to the new mark using heavy-duty scissors or a junior hacksaw. Push the dowels into the cake, keeping them within the diameter of the central column. Cover the largest polystyrene block with 25mm (1in) width ribbon, wrapping it around the block several times to ensure the polystyrene is covered and securing it in position with glue stick. Glue the block to a thin board the same size and shape as (to prevent the dowels pushing through the polystyrene under the weight of the cake). Spread a small amount of royal icing in the centre of the cake.

4 Carefully position the polystyrene block onto the cake (board side facing down), ensuring that the centre of the block is over the central dowel. Repeat with the middle tier and allow both tiers to set for 30 minutes before assembling them. Edge each of the baseboards with 15mm (⅝in) width ribbon and secure it in position with glue stick, ensuring that the ribbon joins on each of the boards and polystyrene blocks is facing the back of the cake. Finally, carefully stack the tiers.

finishing touches

Deciding on suitable decoration for your cake can be a dilemma. The design of cake you choose should befit the occasion and should also be a reflection of the personality of the recipient. Once you have selected a basic design, you can choose to dress the finished cake in many ways.

Fresh flowers are one of my favourite ways to dress a cake, as you will see throughout this book. The effect is instantaneous and dramatic and the scent will enhance any occasion. Fresh flowers can be blocked between tiers without the concern of icing shattering or being damaged and they can complement the tone of the occasion. Fresh flowers can be set into a dome of oasis for protection or simply hand tied. Remove fresh flowers before cutting and serving the cake, as, unless specified, they are not edible.

Silk flowers can safely be packed between tiers, and are an effective alternative to fresh flowers, although they do tend to be more expensive.

Sugar flowers, like silk ones, have the advantage that they can last forever, making ideal keepsakes. However, they are extremely fragile and brittle so reserve them for dressing between tall pillars or fixing to the outside of the cake, as on the cascading lily cake (see pages 120–1).

Fresh fruit adds instant colour and has a great affinity with chocolate – a combination of summer or autumn berries can be piled onto the top of a cake or chocolate-dipped strawberries studded over a chocolate helter-skelter (see pages 136–7).

Sugar butterflies (see pages 124–5) are an effective finishing touch. They can be a mass of bright colours or in soft pastels with shimmers of glitter. Alternatively, look for a variety of silk or lace wired butterflies, doves or dragonflies.

Cute cake toppers add height and humour to a cake. At Little Venice Cake Company we make characters from clay based on photographs supplied by our clients. They are a bespoke keepsake and a lovely reminder of the special occasion. You can also create edible characters from modelling paste or chocolate plastique.

iced cakes

working with icing

This chapter introduces several piping techniques and styles to build up your cake-decorating repertoire. With royal icing, a piping bag and a plain nozzle you can create precision-perfect pearls, ribbon loops, funky candy stripes or delicate lace embroidery. Once you've mastered these techniques, use them to create your own designs.

tiffany pearl ribbon

you will need

6in and 10in square cakes covered with marzipan and sugar paste

13in baseboard covered with icing

piping bags

no. 1.5 nozzle

royal icing

2m (6½ft) length of 12mm (½in) width ribbon to fix around each tier

glue stick (to fix ribbon around baseboard)

1.5m (5ft) length of 15mm (⅝in) width ribbon to edge baseboard

fresh flowers to dress

For a more intimate celebration or wedding anniversary, I like this combination of a 6in cake offset to the back of a 10in square cake positioned on a 13in board. It looks particularly sophisticated with an elegant bunch of burgundy arum lilies. You can transform this design by altering the spacing, size and colour of the pearls.

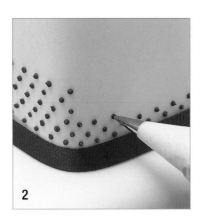

2

1 Stack cakes following instructions on page 35, positioning the base tier towards the back corner of the covered board. Fill a piping bag with a no. 1.5 piping nozzle and fresh royal icing. Fix the ribbon around the base of each tier and around the baseboard. Beginning with the top tier, pipe the first row of pearls just above the ribbon, ensuring that they are evenly positioned.

2 Working on one side of the cake at a time, move the piping bag upwards a few millimetres and pipe the second row of pearls in between the first row. Repeat until you have six rows of pearls on each side of the top tier, then repeat on the base tier. Finally dress the top of the cake with fresh flowers.

full tiffany pearl

you will need

cake covered with marzipan and sugar
paste and placed centrally on a
baseboard 7.5cm (3in) larger

piping bag

no. 2 nozzle

royal icing

12mm (½in) width ribbon for the cake

glue stick

15mm (⅝in) width ribbon to edge
the board

fresh flowers to dress

Here the entire side of the cake is precision piped with pearls. I like to use a slightly larger nozzle and find the whole process rather therapeutic. If you are working on several tiers, always keep one finished tier beside you to ensure that you maintain continuity of the pearl size and spacing. If this is your first attempt, try white pearls on a white cake so that they can be easily removed if you make a mistake.

1 Fill a piping bag with a no. 2 piping nozzle and fresh royal icing. Fix the narrower ribbon around the base of the cake and secure with a dab of royal icing. Glue the wider ribbon around the board. Pipe the first row of pearls just above the ribbon, ensuring that they are evenly positioned and work around the whole tier. (If there is more than one tier, start on the top one.)

2 Moving up a few millimetres, pipe the second row of pearls in between the first row. Complete the whole row before moving on to the next. (It may be a good idea to position the cake on a turntable for this.) Repeat until you reach the top of the cake. Finally, dress the cake with fresh flowers.

cascading pearls

you will need

3-tier cake covered with marzipan and sugar paste and placed on boards the same size as each tier

baseboard 2in larger than base tier, covered with icing

piping bags

no. 3 nozzle

royal icing

12mm (½in) width ribbon to fix around each tier

paintbrush

1 tsp topaz lustre

2 tsp clear piping gel

2 x 5cm (2in) polystyrene blocks, 10cm (4in) smaller than the size of the middle and base tiers

fresh wired flowers

glue stick

15mm (⅝in) width ribbon to edge the baseboard

This design is very simple for the novice cake decorator as there is no pre-marking or structure to follow. Each of the tiers is placed on a board the same size as the cake it supports, so handle the tiers with care, holding them from underneath. I find this cake works particularly well if partnered with strong solid flowers; here I have blocked the cake with a mixture of 'Ecstasy' and 'Aqua' roses, burgundy ranunculus and gloriosa lilies.

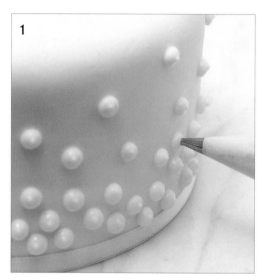

1 Begin with cakes covered and the base tier positioned on the covered board. Fill a piping bag with a no. 3 piping nozzle and fresh royal icing. Fix narrower ribbon around the base of each tier. Begin piping the pearls randomly on each tier, concentrating at the base and making fewer as you move up the side of the cake as shown. Each pearl should have a diameter of approximately 1cm (½in). Use a clean, damp paintbrush to remove the point of each pearl. Repeat on all tiers.

2 Once the icing is dry, the pearls can be brushed with a glaze – use topaz lustre mixed with clear piping gel. Block each tier as shown on page 34 and stud with fresh, wired flowers (see page 53) before stacking the tiers. Finally, glue the wider ribbon around the baseboard.

modern cascading pearls

This elegant square wedding cake has been covered in ivory sugar paste to create smooth soft edges, then hand decorated with cascading pearls in white royal icing. I have included a border of pearls around the base for a special finishing touch. The pearls have been glazed with a clear edible gel so they glisten and the finished cake dressed with fresh white lilies.

3-tier caramel ribbon loops

Individual hand-iced ribbon loops can also be used to decorate a stacked, tiered cake. For this cake I have used a combination of white, ivory and caramel loops on an ivory-covered cake. The tiers are stacked and surrounded with 25mm (1in) width gold ribbon before the loops are fixed into position at an angle around each tier with royal icing. I have presented this cake on a contemporary square board.

ribbon loops

you will need

5cm (2in) cube cakes covered with marzipan and sugar paste

12mm (½in) width ribbon for fixing around each cake

coloured and white royal icing

piping bags

no. 3 nozzles

heavy-duty waxed paper

iced boards

15mm (⅝in) width ribbon for edging boards

glue stick

7.5cm- (3in-) high polystyrene columns

You can create extremely versatile designs using fresh royal icing and a plain nozzle. This cake is a novel display of individual cakes, each dressed with hand-piped, royal-iced ribbon loops.

1 Attach a length of 12mm (½in) ribbon around each cake, securing it with a dab of royal icing at the back of the cake. Using a piping bag fitted with a no. 3 nozzle and filled with coloured royal icing, pipe a series of double loops onto heavy-duty waxed paper (shiny side up). Repeat using other colours. You will need about 6 double loops for each individual cake. Allow to dry overnight.

2 Pipe a small dome of stiff white royal icing on top of each individual iced cake. Carefully peel the iced ribbon loops off the waxed paper and fix in position. Work on one cake at a time and ensure all the loops are facing towards the middle.

To assemble Arrange the finished cakes on an iced stand made with square boards edged in 15mm (⅝in) width ribbon and 7.5cm- (3in-) high polystyrene columns (see page 32).

candy stripes

you will need

8in round cake covered with marzipan and sugar paste and placed centrally on an 11in board covered with sugar paste

white royal icing and 3 bright food colours

piping bags fitted with no. 3 nozzles

scribe

8in round board

15mm (⅝in) width ribbon for the board

fresh flowers to dress

This candy-stripe cake design, hand piped with vertical pinstripes in three bright colours, is eye-catching and fun. Changing the colours to complement the theme or flowers of an occasion is an effective way to completely transform the design. It can be adapted to create a feminine birthday cake, or made bold and bright for a more funky look. I have also used this technique for christening cakes in shades of blue and pink.

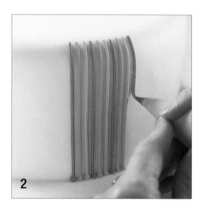

1 Divide 1 quantity of fresh royal icing into 3 clean bowls and colour each portion to the desired intensity. Spoon the icing into 3 separate piping bags, each fitted with a no. 3 nozzle.

2 Using a scribe, mark around an 8in board positioned carefully on top of an iced 8in cake, to act as the top guide. Pipe one icing colour in a vertical line from the top guide to the cake board. Pipe the second colour parallel to the first and the third colour parallel to the second. Repeat all the way around the cake.

3 Fix ribbon around the edge of the baseboard and dress the top of the finished cake with fresh flowers or a simple piped message, if desired.

3-tier funky candy stripe

As a tiered cake this candy stripe design is particularly dazzling. Here I have combined purple, ruby and yellow candy stripes with fresh tulips, anemones and roses.

catlia lace

you will need

3-tier round cake – 4in/6in/8in tiers covered with marzipan and white sugar paste, stacked centrally on an 11in round board covered with white sugar paste

350g (12oz) white sugar paste to make the ribbon bands

icing sugar

rolling pin

sharp knife

ruler

pastry brush

template (see page 154)

greaseproof paper

pen

scribe

piping bags

no. 1.5 and no. 3 nozzle

white royal icing

paintbrush

topaz lustre mixed with alcohol dipping solution

1m (40in) length of 15mm (⅝in) width white ribbon to edge the baseboard

The inspiration for this cake comes from an exquisite piece of lace ribbon. I have adapted the design to work around an iced ribbon band on this small, three-tier stacked cake. The finished cake is presented on a polystyrene block studded with fresh roses to create additional height and drama.

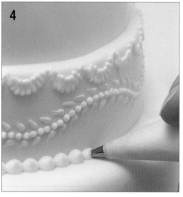

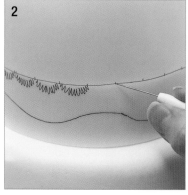

Tip When using a template with a repeating pattern to mark up several tiers, work from the base tier upwards. This way you can use just one template, cutting it shorter for the upper tiers. Make sure the join of the design is always at the back of the cake. When decorating a tiered cake, always begin with the top tier and work downwards so the icing is not smudged or damaged.

1 Knead the white sugar paste until smooth and pliable. Divide into 3 portions (adjusting for the different sizes of tiers). Lightly dust a work surface with icing sugar and roll out a ribbon of icing sufficient to fit all the way around the top tier. Cut the iced ribbon using a knife and ruler to create straight edges top and bottom. Moisten the base of the tier with water and fix the iced ribbon band in position as shown. Repeat with other tiers making sure all the iced ribbon bands join at the back of the cake. Allow to set overnight.

2 Using the template on page 154, trace enough of the lace design onto greaseproof paper to fit around the base tier. With the template in position, use a scribe to prick the design onto the sugar paste ribbon. Repeat with the middle and top tiers.

3 Fill a piping bag with a no. 1.5 nozzle and white royal icing. Pipe the scallops around the top edge of the ribbon, then the central strand of pearls with tiny leaves on each side as shown. Finish with a pearl at the top of each scallop.

4 Fill a piping bag with a no. 3 nozzle and white royal icing. Pipe large pearls around the base of each tier. When the icing is dry, brush the scallops and pearl strand and leaves with topaz lustre mixed with alcohol dipping solution. Fix ribbon around the baseboard, securing it with a dab of royal icing at the back.

preparing flowers for blocking

you will need

florist's scissors

fresh roses

florist's wires cut to 10cm (4in) lengths

9cm (3½in) deep round polystyrene base
(allows 2 rows of roses)

I like to dress cakes with fresh flowers. There are many varieties and colours available so it is worth experimenting, but I have found roses to be particularly effective for blocking between tiers of a cake or for studding a polystyrene base for display, as here.

1 Trim each rose to leave approximately 2cm (¾in) of stalk. Gently tease a wire into the stalk.

2 Insert the wire into the polystyrene block. Repeat, working around the cake base or tier and ensure the roses are lined up and equal.

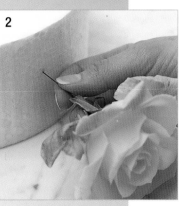

The following table is provided as a guide only. The numbers will vary depending on the species of rose, how full blown the flowers are and how tightly you position them next to one another. You may like to include other flowers or greenery to fill any gaps and reduce the cost.

Size of tier	Number of roses required	
	Single row	Double row
6in	8	14
8in	12	22
10in	16	30
12in	20	38
14in	26	50
16in	32	60

Tip For a single row of roses and flowers allow 5cm (2in) between the tiers; for a double row allow 9cm (3½in) and position the upper row in between the flowers on the bottom row. Don't underestimate the number of flowers you will need!

lace brush embroidery

you will need

3-tier cake covered with marzipan and sugar paste and stacked centrally on a baseboard 7.5cm (3in) larger than base tier, covered with sugar paste

piping bags

no. 2 nozzle

royal icing

25mm (1in) width ribbon to fix around each tier

template (see page 149), optional

paintbrush

topaz lustre mixed with dipping alcohol solution

15mm (⅝in) width ribbon to edge baseboard

glue stick (to fix ribbon around baseboard)

fresh rose petals to dress (optional)

A cake covered in delicate hand-iced lace is extremely romantic. I love this design, which was inspired by the handmade lace featured on my own wedding dress. It is essentially made up of three patterns – a large flower, which is brush embroidered, smaller flowers and clusters of berries with leaves – which are repeated randomly over the cake ensuring all the space is filled. It is a good idea to practise piping a section of the lace design onto a spare cake board to get a feel for the pattern before you begin piping it freehand onto the cake.

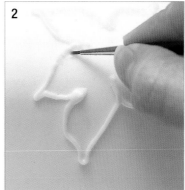

Tip Fix the ribbon around each tier first and pipe the design on each tier up to the edge of the ribbon. This allows the ribbon to settle flush against the smooth icing on the covered cake.

1 Fill a piping bag with a no. 2 nozzle and royal icing. Fix ribbon around the base of each tier. Starting on the top tier hand pipe a small section of the lace design. Pipe the design freehand or use the template on page 149 if you wish.

2 Each time you have piped a large flower, stop and, using a clean, damp paintbrush, gently brush the inner edge only of the piped line towards the centre. Work in small sections over each tier, moving downwards and filling in all the spaces until the whole cake is covered.

3 Once the icing is dry, the whole design can be brushed with a glaze – use topaz lustre mixed with alcohol dipping solution. Fix ribbon around the baseboard. If desired, dress the cake with fresh rose petals.

hand-painted orchid

you will need

4-tier round cake – 4in/6in/8in/10in tiers covered with marzipan and ivory sugar paste and stacked centrally

13in and 16in round baseboards covered with ivory sugar paste

templates (see page 147)

tracing paper

pen

scribe

10g (⅓oz) cocoa butter

edible colour dusts

paintbrush

3m (10ft) length of 15mm (⅝in) width purple ribbon

royal icing (to fix ribbon around tiers)

4m (13ft) length of 9mm (⅜in) width purple ribbon

glue stick (to fix ribbon around baseboard)

fresh flowers to dress

Painting onto a cake indulges two of my passions in one! I find it very satisfying both to paint and to create a truly individual decorated cake. I took the inspiration for this orchid cake from a wall-hanging that I have at home. The design is traced and etched onto the cake with layers of edible colour dusts suspended in cocoa butter – a bit like painting in oils. Change the flowers, positions or colours to design your own cake.

Tip If you make a mistake while painting, simply absorb the cocoa butter and colour with a clean piece of paper towel.

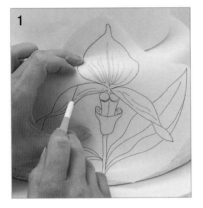

1 Cover the cakes 2 days before decorating and stack the tiers the day before. Trace the orchid and butterfly designs separately onto tracing paper using a pen. Cut each design out and decide where you would like each one to be positioned on the cake, working upwards with the largest flower on the base tier. Carefully hold the tracing paper against the cake and use a scribe to mark the design onto the cake. (By gently dragging the scribe over the design it will form an indentation that will be visible when you remove the paper.) Repeat with all the flowers and butterflies. Use a scribe to join the flowers up with a central stalk.

2 Melt the cocoa butter in a saucer suspended over a heat-resistant bowl of boiling water. Tip various edible colour dusts onto the edge of the saucer. Use a paintbrush to gently mix the cocoa butter with the colour dusts and paint onto the cake. (The more cocoa butter you use, the more translucent the paint colours will be.) Build up colours and layers gradually, allowing time for each to set as the cocoa butter cools. If the cocoa butter starts to cool and harden on the saucer, replace the boiling water in the bowl underneath.

To assemble Once the design is finished and dry, fix the narrower ribbon around each tier, securing it in position at the back of each cake with a dab of royal icing. Glue the wider ribbon around the baseboards. Dress the cake with fresh flowers, such as Vanda orchids.

ballerina fairy

you will need

8in petal-shaped cake covered with marzipan and sugar paste

11in petal-shaped board covered with sugar paste

12mm (½in) width ribbon for the cake

6 medium stamped-out flowers

15mm (⅝in) width ribbon for the board

glue stick (for fixing ribbon around board)

templates (see page 149)

tracing paper

pen

scribe

10g (⅓oz) cocoa butter

edible colour dusts

paintbrush

piping bag

no. 1.5 nozzle

55g (2oz) white royal icing

topaz lustre

edible hologram glitter

alcohol dipping solution

Using brush embroidery over a hand-painted design is a versatile way to build up depth. I have two goddaughters and three nieces who particularly approve of this design, which features a sophisticated fairy ballerina together with her fairy dust and army of bumble bees.

1 Position the cake centrally on the covered board. Fix the narrower ribbon around the cake, securing it with royal icing at the back and in each of the indentations of the petal shape. Position a stamped-out flower in each of the indentations of the petal over the ribbon as shown. Fix the wider ribbon around the baseboard. Trace the fairy ballerina and bumble bee designs onto tracing paper. Gently hold the design against the cake and use a scribe to mark the design onto the cake.

2 Melt the cocoa butter in a saucer suspended over a heat-resistant bowl of boiling water. Tip colour dusts onto the edge of the saucer. Use a paintbrush to gently mix the cocoa butter with the colour dusts as desired and paint onto the cake. Build up colours and layers, allowing time for each to set as the cocoa butter cools. If the cocoa butter starts to cool and harden on the saucer, replace the boiling water in the bowl underneath.

3 Fill a piping bag with a no. 1.5 nozzle and fresh white royal icing. Pipe around the outline of the fairy's skirt and the wings of the bumble bees. Use a damp paintbrush to gently brush the icing line inwards to create a brush embroidery effect. Pipe tiny pearls at the fairy's fingers to resemble fairy dust. Allow to dry. Mix a little topaz lustre with edible hologram glitter and enough alcohol dipping solution to create a thin paste. Brush over the royal icing with a paintbrush.

birds of paradise

you will need

2-tier hexagonal cake covered with marzipan and caramel-ivory coloured sugar paste

baseboard 7.5cm (3in) larger than base tier, covered with sugar paste

12mm (½in) width ribbon to fix around cake tiers and edge the baseboard

royal icing (for fixing ribbon around cake tiers and baseboard)

templates (see page 148)

tracing paper

pen

scribe

10g (⅓oz) cocoa butter

edible colour dusts

paintbrush

fresh flowers to dress

I was inspired by the beautiful detail on a silk brisé fan for this design, which is full of Eastern promise and romance, befitting a special wedding or anniversary cake. I have chosen to paint with earth and spice tones of saffron, basil, ochre and burnt sienna and to dress the cake with fresh golden-shower orchids and gloriosa lilies.

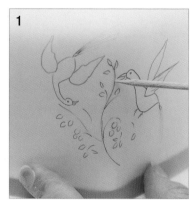

1 Stack the cakes and position on the baseboard, following the instructions on page 35. Fix the ribbon around the base of each tier and around the baseboard, securing with royal icing at the back. Trace the birds of paradise designs (see page 148) separately onto tracing paper using a pen. Gently hold the template against the cake and use a scribe to mark the design onto the cake.

2 Melt the cocoa butter in a saucer suspended over a heat-resistant bowl of boiling water. Tip colour dusts onto the edge of the saucer. Use a paintbrush to gently mix the cocoa butter with the colour dusts as desired and paint onto the cake. Build up colours and layers gradually, allowing time for each to set as the cocoa butter cools. Finally, dress the cake with fresh flowers.

Tip If the cocoa butter starts to cool and harden on the saucer, replace the boiling water in the bowl underneath.

woven ribbon

you will need

8in round cake covered with marzipan and hot-pink sugar paste, placed on an 11in round board covered with sugar paste

glue stick

1.5m (5ft) length of 15mm (⅝in) width citrus-green ribbon

royal icing

piping bag

3m (10ft) length of 3mm (⅛in) width citrus-green ribbon

ruler

white paper

pen

sharp scissors

scribe

ribbon-insertion tool

fresh flowers to dress

The first time I saw ribbon inserted into a cake I was convinced that the ribbon had literally been threaded through the icing. In fact, this is an illusion: little snippets of ribbon are actually tucked into pre-marked slits. It's an extremely effective and relatively simple way to decorate a cake. This triple-looped design works well on a round cake and looks very striking as a tiered wedding cake. The ribbon loops are topped with handmade ribbon bows in the same colour. I have used numerous colours of ribbon on many different coloured cakes – but this is definitely the first time for hot pink and citrus green!

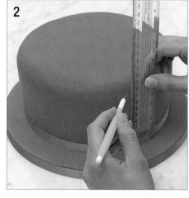

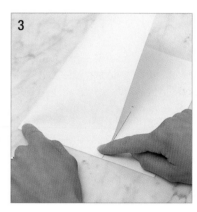

Tip If you're using this design on a multi-tiered cake, make sure that you keep the base point of the loops the same on each cake (you can adjust the top height of the loops if necessary).

1 Allow the covered cake to dry overnight before decorating it. Glue 15mm (⅝in) width ribbon around the edge of the baseboard. Fix 15mm (⅝in) width ribbon around the base of the cake, securing the join at the back with royal icing. Measure the circumference of the cake by wrapping 3mm (⅛in) width ribbon around the cake, then holding the length of ribbon against a ruler. Divide this length by 3 to give you the distance between each ribbon loop.

2 Hold a ruler against the cake and measure from the base of the cake to the height you want the top of the ribbon loops to be (ideally they should be approximately 1cm/½in from the top of the cake). Similarly, measure the lowest point of the loop (about 2cm/¾in from the base, depending on the overall height of the cake).

3 Measuring from the corner of a clean piece of paper, mark the height of the top of the ribbon loop along one edge. Fold over the edge of the paper at this point to form a strip. Carefully cut the strip from the rest of the sheet of paper, then mark the distance between the ribbon loops on the long edge of the paper strip. Cut off the remainder of the strip. Fold the strip of paper in half crosswise.

4 Mark the lowest point of the ribbon loop on the folded edge of the paper strip, then draw half a loop/arc freehand reaching from the lowest point at the fold up to the top of the opposite outside edge.

5 Cut along the line of the loop/arc. Open out the paper to show a perfectly symmetrical loop.

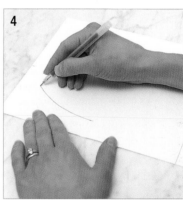

6 Hold the template against the cake and use a scribe to trace the loop onto the cake, starting at the top of the loop. Repeat twice more and the loops should join up at the back of the cake.

7 Working from left to right, use the ribbon-insertion tool to follow the line of the loops, firmly pressing it into the cake until the base touches the scribed line. Insert the left-hand prong into the last slit made. This will ensure the slits are evenly spaced. Continue all around the cake.

8 Cut some 2cm (1in) lengths from 3mm (⅛in) width ribbon. Starting at the top of a loop, use the ribbon-insertion tool to tuck the left-hand side of the ribbon in first. Fold ribbon over the second slit and push in snugly. Repeat around the cake.

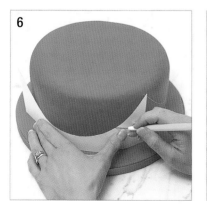

To assemble Make 3 simple ribbon bows from the remainder of the ribbon and fix them into position at the top of the loops with royal icing. Finally, dress the top of the cake with fresh flowers.

chocolate cakes

chocolate

Chocolate cakes are visually stunning and decadent. They are also generally sculptured and therefore less precise than iced cakes. This can be very appealing to less experienced – and more expressive – cake decorators, as most of these cakes are created without piping bags and nozzles.

tempering chocolate

I like to cover individual cakes with pure melted chocolate. The taste and finish is a clean, crisp chocolate with all the appeal of a decadent chocolate truffle. However, in order to work effectively with melted chocolate it must first be tempered (or pre-crystallized) to achieve the shine, correct melting properties and stability of quality chocolate. Most importantly, tempering chocolate will prevent blooming (unsightly white streaks in the chocolate as it resets).

3

1 Break the chocolate into small pieces and place in a large clean bowl over a pan of simmering water. (Do not boil – if water or steam comes into contact with the chocolate, it will turn into a solid block. Water and chocolate do not mix!) Stir the chocolate while melting to ensure even heating but try to avoid creating air bubbles. Heat chocolate to 45°C (113°F).

2 Replace the hot water with cold water and stir continuously until the chocolate cools to 27°C (81°F). Occasionally it may be necessary to add additional cool water underneath the bowl.

3 Now replace the cold water with warm water and raise the temperature of the chocolate to between 31°C and 32°C (89–90°F) for dark chocolate, 30°C and 31°C (86–89°F) for milk chocolate and 28°C and 29°C (82–84°F) for white chocolate. Maintain the appropriate temperature while dipping. If the chocolate cools or warms outside of these temperatures, you will need to repeat the tempering process.

4 Test the temper of the chocolate before starting to dip. This can be done by spreading a small amount onto aluminium foil and allowing it to cool. It should be smooth and shiny with no dull or wet areas. Streaks may indicate poor temper or a lack of mixing. If the results are unsatisfactory, you will need to retemper the chocolate before proceeding.

Tip The room used for tempering and dipping chocolate should be 20°C (68°F) and draught free. If the room or chocolate is too warm, the chocolates may have large 'tailings' or feet. If the chocolate becomes too warm or too cool it will lack shine or show signs of bloom. Low humidity, no strong odours and good air circulation are also recommended. Having a good thermometer with a range from 16°C to 50°C (60–122°F) is advisable.

poured chocolate ganache icing

For a decadent covering for the chocolate truffle or luscious lemon cakes, pour smooth chocolate ganache icing over a cake that has been sandwiched, surrounded and topped with buttercream. This recipe differs slightly from the chocolate ganache I blend with buttercream for the filling in that I have added butter, which allows the ganache icing to pour smoothly and remain glossy.

dark chocolate ganache icing

you will need

500g (1lb 2oz) dark chocolate (70% cocoa solids), broken into pieces

250g (9oz) unsalted butter, cut into small pieces

125ml (4½fl oz) double cream

yields 850g (1lb 14oz)

1 Place the chocolate and butter in a bowl. In a pan, bring cream to the boil and pour over chocolate and butter. Stir with a wooden spoon until chocolate and butter have melted and icing is smooth.

2 While it is still warm, pour the ganache liberally over a prepared cake standing on a wire rack set on a piece of non-stick baking paper. Use a palette knife or the back of a metal spoon to move the chocolate over the cake top and sides. Holding the rack with both hands, gently tap it to allow the ganache icing to even itself and settle over the cake.

1

2

To store Spoon any excess ganache into a container and store in the refrigerator for up to 2 weeks. Ganache is suitable for freezing for up to 1 month: allow it to defrost overnight at room temperature, then gently heat in a microwave or in a bowl over simmering water.

size of cake	6in	8in	10in	12in
quantity of ganache to cover	½ quantity	1 quantity	1½ quantity	2 quantity

white chocolate ganache icing

Heat the cream until it has just boiled to avoid a skim on the top of the cream. (If you overboil it, pour it over the chocolate through a sieve.) Pour over white chocolate and stir until smooth. Adding melted butter will create a higher gloss to the icing, but is not essential.

you will need

250ml (9fl oz) double cream

500g (1lb 2oz) white chocolate, pellets or chopped

1–2tbsp unsalted butter, melted (optional)

yields 750g (1lb 11oz)

chocolate plastique

Chocolate plastique is a combination of pure chocolate with a sugar stock syrup– effectively glucose – which makes chocolate malleable, enabling you to roll it out to cover a cake or hand mould it to create the fans, roses and leaves used in many of the designs shown here. Chocolate plastique has all the taste of chocolate, but with the texture of sugar paste and gives a smooth, firm finish to a cake. You can use chocolate plastique to cover a cake in exactly the same way as you would marzipan and sugar paste: follow quantities given for marzipan for a single layer and for sugar paste for a second layer (see pages 25 and 27). To make milk chocolate plastique, knead together dark and white chocolate plastique.

stock syrup

you will need

250ml (9fl oz) water

140g (5oz) caster sugar

85g (3oz) glucose syrup

yields 450ml (16fl oz)

Place all the ingredients into a saucepan and bring to the boil. Remove from the heat and leave to cool. This recipe will provide slightly more than necessary to create the white chocolate plastique recipe below.

white chocolate plastique

you will need

1.75kg (3lb 14oz) white chocolate, broken into pieces

115g (4oz) cocoa butter

400g (14oz) glucose syrup

300ml (10fl oz) stock syrup

yields 2½kg (5½lb)

1 Melt the chocolate in a microwave or place it in a clean, heat-resistant bowl over a saucepan of simmering water. Melt the cocoa butter in a microwave or place it in a clean, heat-resistant bowl over a saucepan of simmering water. (It is important to melt the cocoa butter and chocolate separately as they melt at different rates and both need to be melted for the recipe to work.) Mix the chocolate and cocoa butter together and stir well. Measure the glucose syrup and stock syrup together and warm slightly in the microwave. (This allows all the ingredients to be at a similar temperature for the final mix.)

2

Tip If the paste is very stiff, place in a microwave for 10 seconds on medium heat to soften. If it is too soft or warm, refrigerate it for a couple of minutes to harden slightly.

2 Pour chocolate over glucose and stock syrups and mix well with a wooden spoon until smooth. Transfer the mixture into a clean large freezer bag and leave overnight at room temperature to set.

3 When ready to use, knead the chocolate plastique until smooth and pliable. Roll out on a work surface lightly dusted with icing sugar.

3

dark chocolate plastique

you will need

1.25kg (2lb 12oz) dark chocolate, 55% maximum cocoa solids, broken into pieces

1kg (2lb 4oz) glucose syrup

yields 2.25kg (5lb)

Melt the chocolate in a microwave or place it in a clean, heat-resistant bowl over a pan of simmering water. Heat to 43°C (110°F). Heat the glucose syrup separately to the same temperature. Pour the syrup into the melted chocolate and stir with a wooden spoon until thoroughly combined. Allow to cool completely. Transfer the mixture into a clean large freezer bag and leave overnight at room temperature to set. To use, peel away the bag and knead the chocolate until smooth and pliable.

piping chocolate

Piping with chocolate is similar to piping with royal icing. You can use either pure, melted, tempered chocolate or a cooled, poured chocolate ganache.

piping melted chocolate

For pure melted chocolate it is not advisable to use a nozzle, as the chocolate tends to set as it comes into contact with the stainless steel of the nozzle, causing it to clog up. Simply fill a piping bag with melted chocolate and snip the end. Use this technique to pipe messages onto cakes or to create chocolate decorations. To make the ones shown opposite, pipe a central loop onto waxed paper (shiny side up). Still holding the bag, pipe a second loop lower and outside of the first. Repeat with 2 more loops – always coming back to the base centre. Allow the decorations to cool before carefully peeling them off the waxed paper.

piping chocolate ganache

The cooled ganache used for pouring over a cake (see page 67) also works very well for piping. It flows well through a piping bag filled with a nozzle. Fill a bag with a plain no. 4 nozzle to create large pearls around the base of a cake. Use various nozzles to create scrolls, stars and flowers and other decorations as shown. If the ganache becomes too stiff to pipe, gently heat it in a microwave or in a bowl over simmering water for a few moments before continuing.

chocolate glazing lustres

Chocolate can be dusted with glazing lustre to add colour to the finished cake. Lustres are available in many colours including copper, bronze, sapphire, ruby, jade, gold and topaz. Use a paintbrush to brush the powder lustres onto hand-moulded chocolate-plastique roses, leaves and fans to develop the colour.

adding lustre to a chocolate cake

Lustres can be added to whole cakes, such as this dark chocolate-plastique helter-skelter, to provide a metallic sheen. Dark chocolate picks up the strong lustre colours particularly well. As with small chocolate decorations, simply brush the powders on with a large paintbrush while the chocolate is still fresh. You can also add lustres to a cake freshly covered in a poured dark chocolate ganache. Gently flick a paintbrush of lustre across one corner of the top of the cake before dressing it with hand-moulded chocolate roses and leaves and/or fresh fruit.

chocolate ganache torte

you will need

8in chocolate truffle torte, layered with chocolate ganache buttercream and fresh raspberries, placed on an 8in board

wire rack

non-stick baking paper

ladle

1 quantity poured chocolate ganache (see page 67)

palette knife

piping bag

no. 4 nozzle

fresh berries and hand-moulded chocolate roses (see page 75) to decorate

The chocolate truffle torte here is layered with chocolate ganache buttercream and fresh raspberries with lashings of poured chocolate ganache. To finish I have dressed the cake with fresh berries and hand-moulded chocolate roses.

1 Place the prepared cake on a wire rack over a sheet of non-stick baking paper. Liberally pour ladlefuls of the chocolate ganache over the cake. Make gentle circular swirls with the base of the ladle over the ganache to encourage it to run down and coat the sides of the cake.

2 Gently hold the sides of the wire rack, lift it up and tap it down gently but firmly to level the ganache and remove any air bubbles. Use a palette knife to ensure the top and sides are evenly coated and textured.

3 Lift the cake off the wire rack using a palette knife and set on a serving plate. Fill a piping bag with a large plain nozzle and 2 large spoonfuls of the chocolate ganache. Pipe beads of chocolate around the base of the cake to neaten the edges. Dress the top of the cake with fresh berries and hand-moulded chocolate roses.

Tip For a wedding cake, pour the ganache over the cake but rather than using a palette knife, allow the ganache to find its own level to create a smooth finish. You may like to first cover the tiers with an initial coat of white chocolate plastique for a professional touch.

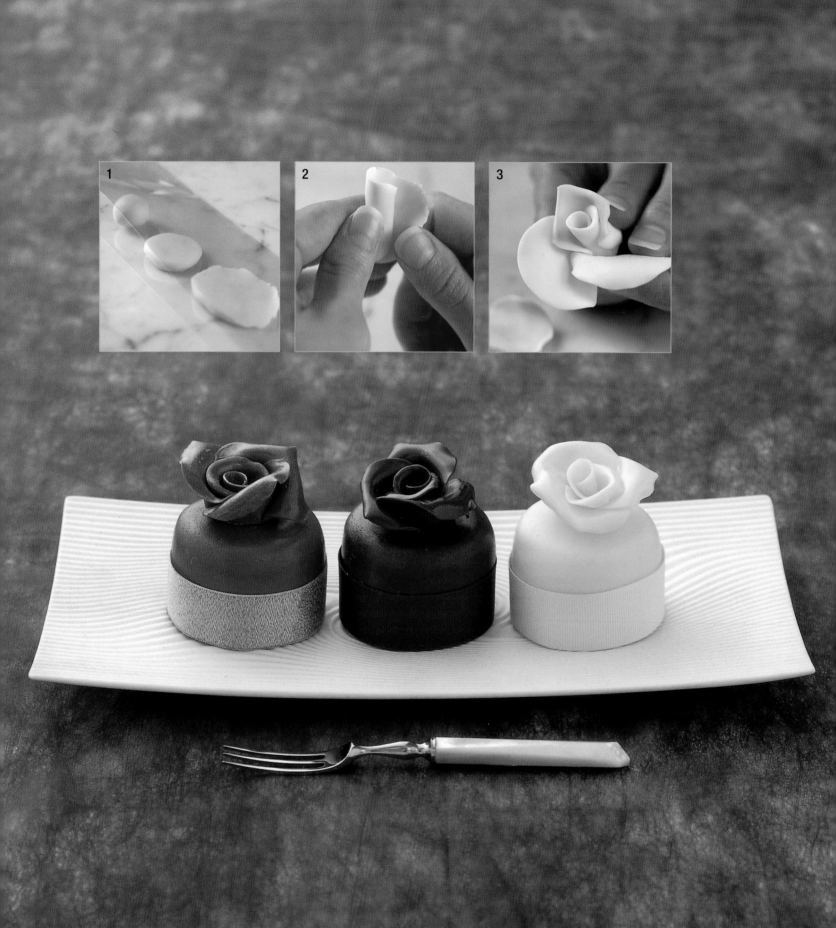

chocolate roses

you will need

3 x 2in round individual cakes

100g (3½oz) each of white, dark and milk chocolate plastique

plastic sheeting

palette knife

3 x 20cm (8in) lengths of 15mm (⅝in) width cream, gold and dark brown grosgrain ribbon

25g (1oz) white chocolate, melted

25g (1oz) dark chocolate, melted

piping bags

Individual chocolate-covered cakes look stunning dressed with these hand-moulded chocolate roses. They are perfect for an elegant wedding, served for pudding dressed on a plate with a little raspberry coulis or coconut ice cream. The quantity of chocolate plastique given here will make approximately 8–10 roses of 5cm (2in) diameter or cover three mini cakes and make a rose for the top of each as shown opposite. The roses will store well for up to six months in a cool, dry container.

1 Warm a small amount of chocolate plastique between your palms and roll into a ball. Place between 2 sheets of plastic. Flatten quickly with the base of your palm, then, using your index finger, flatten two-thirds of the way round the ball, leaving a thicker base.

2 Remove the chocolate from the plastic sheeting and, holding the thicker base, gently roll the chocolate to form the centre of the rose.

3 Repeat step 1 to create 4 more petals. Wrap a petal around the rose centre, then fix the final 3 petals so they overlap one another. Gently tease the petals into shape. Slice the base off the finished rose using a palette knife.

To assemble Cover each cake with a double layer of white, milk or dark chocolate plastique. Attach ribbon around the base of each cake, securing with melted chocolate. Pipe a small amount of melted chocolate onto the base of the chocolate roses and fix into position on the cakes.

Tip This method for hand-moulding chocolate roses can also be used for making roses from sugar paste.

individual chocolate rose stand

Set a number of individual chocolate-rose-decorated cakes on a stand for a special occasion. Here I have added a 6in top tier for the cutting ceremony. These cakes are shelf stable and will not spoil if left out of the refrigerator throughout a reception.

tricolore fans and roses

you will need

3-tier cake – 4in/7in/10in cakes covered
with white, milk and dark chocolate
plastique respectively, placed on boards
the same size and stacked centrally

13in baseboard covered with
dark chocolate plastique

white, milk and dark chocolate to fix
the roses and fans into position

900g (2lb) white chocolate plastique

1.4kg (3lb) dark chocolate plastique

icing sugar

rolling pin

hand-moulded chocolate roses –
12 white, 16 milk and 20 dark chocolate
(see page 75)

15mm (⅝in) width brown
grosgrain ribbon

This chocolate creation is an adaptation of the wedding cake I designed and created for Sir Paul McCartney and Heather Mills. Each tier of the cake is covered in chocolate then adorned with hand-moulded roses and fans. The effect is an amazing sculpture of chocolate that needs no further decoration of fruit or flowers.

1 Melt the chocolates separately. Knead the chocolate plastique until smooth and pliable. Use 375g (13oz) each of white and dark plastique to make milk chocolate plastique. Lightly dust a work surface with icing sugar and roll each of the 3 types of plastique to a large square 5mm (¼in) thick. Cut out rectangles of varying sizes. Take a rectangle of plastique and concertina it. Pinch the centre and fold in half to make a fan.

2 Beginning with the base tier, fix the dark chocolate roses and fans in position with melted dark chocolate. Allow the fans and roses to protrude over the top edge of the cake tier but do not curl them inwards.

3 Repeat with the milk chocolate middle tier and finish with the white chocolate fans and roses on the top tier. As long as there is no fresh fruit inside the cake it can remain in this state stored in a cool dry place (but not refrigerated) for up to 3 days. Edge the board with ribbon once the cake is decorated.

white velvet rose

you will need

3-tier cake – 4in/7in/10in tiers, covered with white chocolate plastique and placed on boards the same size

13in and 16in boards covered with white chocolate plastique

100g (3½oz) white chocolate, melted

piping bag

250 (approx) white chocolate scrolls

40 hand-moulded white chocolate fans (see page 76)

30 hand-moulded white chocolate roses (see page 75)

15mm (⅝in) width cream grosgrain ribbon to edge baseboards

fresh rose petals to dress (optional)

Chocolate scrolls or cigarillos will transform a simple chocolate cake into a truly spectacular one. They are commercially available in white and dark chocolate and handle extremely well. The cake should be initially prepared with buttercream and covered with a layer of ganache (single tier) or chocolate plastique (multiple tiers).

size of square tier	number of scrolls (approx.)
4in	50
6in	75
8in	100
10in	120
12in	150
14in	170
16in	200

Tip The hand-moulded roses can be made well in advance, but make the fans as you go, using them to fill any gaps.

1 Place the base tier onto the double baseboards, fixing into position with melted chocolate. Fill a piping bag with melted white chocolate. Snip the end off the bag and, working on a 10cm (4in) section at a time, pipe trails of chocolate onto the sides of the cake. Stick chocolate scrolls onto the cake evenly with joins against the cake. Repeat until all tiers are surrounded and leave until the chocolate has set firm.

2 When you are ready to dress the cake, stack the tiers as shown on page 35, fixing them into position with a little melted white chocolate. Working on one tier at a time, position the white chocolate fans and roses around the tiers, finishing with a flourish on the top tier. Attach ribbon around the baseboards, securing it with melted chocolate at the back of the cake. Dress the base of the cake with fresh rose petals, if desired.

chocolate scroll birthday

For a truly decadent birthday cake, decorate a chocolate truffle torte with dark chocolate scrolls. Position a sugar paste plaque in the centre of the cake and decorate with fresh seasonal berries.

individual ganache bites

These individual bite-size cakes are covered with an initial coat of white chocolate plastique then enrobed with tempered chocolate. Each is topped with a chocolate-dipped strawberry and displayed on a white chocolate stand. This cake is very popular for cocktail parties, for which the little cakes are an ideal size. Be sure to make enough! I use a half-depth cake to make these bites. This keeps the height down so they are easier to eat with your fingers.

you will need

8in single-layer square chocolate truffle torte, split in half horizontally and sandwiched with chocolate ganache buttercream (yields 25 bites)

8in square luscious lemon cake split in half horizontally, one half split again and sandwiched with lemon curd buttercream (yields 25 bites)

4cm (1½in) and 5cm (2in) round cutters

pastry brush

300g (10½oz) apricot jam

rolling pin

1.5kg (3lb 8oz) white chocolate plastique

wire rack

non-stick baking paper

1kg (2lb 4oz) white chocolate

small ladle or spoon

piping bag

1kg (2lb 4oz) dark chocolate

50 small strawberries

waxed paper

3-tier white chocolate stand

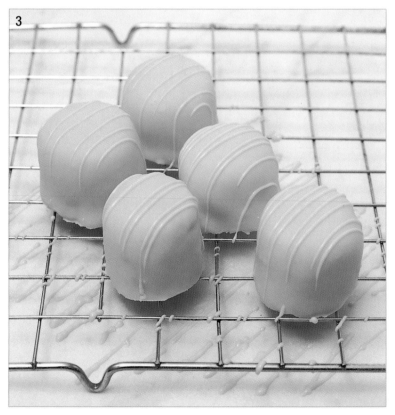

1 Cut rounds of cake using a 4cm (1½in) cutter and brush each small cake with apricot jam.

2 Cover each cake with a single layer of white chocolate plastique. (Use the larger cutter to trim excess.) Keep the chocolate and lemon cakes separate. Working on batches of 5–8 at a time, place the prepared chocolate cakes on a wire rack over a sheet of non-stick baking paper.

3 Temper white chocolate and pour spoonfuls over the lemon cakes. Excess chocolate can be reused. Fill a piping bag with white chocolate and snip the end. Using a piping bag with the end snipped off, drizzle white chocolate over the cakes in a criss-cross design. Temper the dark chocolate and repeat the above to cover and decorate chocolate cakes.

To assemble Dip strawberries in tempered chocolate and allow to set on waxed paper. Present the bites on a chocolate stand with a chocolate-dipped strawberry placed on each.

cakes for events

valentine heart

you will need

10in heart-shaped cake covered with dark chocolate (poured ganache or chocolate plastique), placed on a board the same shape and size or on a serving plate

100g (3½oz) dark chocolate (if cake is covered with chocolate plastique)

piping bag

120 (approx) dark chocolate scrolls

1kg (2¼lb) strawberries

10 (approx) dark chocolate decorative pieces (see page 70)

1.5m (5ft) length of red organza ribbon

Oh, the romance, the seduction, the decadence! I have used a heart-shaped tin to bake this chocolate truffle torte and layered the tiers with chocolate ganache buttercream and fresh sliced strawberries. The cake is surrounded with dark chocolate scrolls and the top packed with fresh strawberries and hand-piped chocolate decorations. Serve it, ideally for breakfast, with a glass of chilled pink champagne – your Valentine will be spellbound!

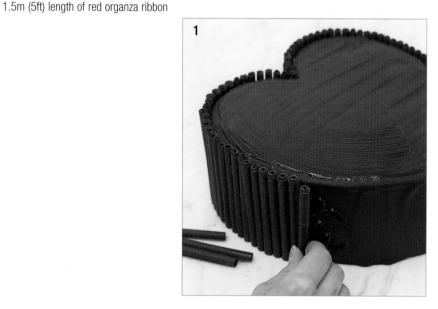

1 If the cake has been covered in dark chocolate plastique, melt the dark chocolate and pour into a piping bag. Snip the end off the bag and pipe a trail of dark chocolate over a 10cm (4in) section of the side of the cake. Fix scrolls into position with the join on each scroll touching the cake. Work all the way around the cake.

2 Brush the top of the cake with melted chocolate and gently set the fresh strawberries into position. Use the chocolate decorative pieces to fill any small gaps. To finish, tie the cake with a red organza ribbon and bow.

Tip If you cover the cake with poured ganache you will not need the melted chocolate to stick the scrolls into position – they will adhere to the ganache. Always use chocolate plastique rather than ganache to cover a multi-tier cake as it is more stable.

rosebud heart

you will need

3-tier heart cake – 6in/9in/12in tiers covered with ivory sugar paste and stacked centrally

15in and 18in heart-shaped baseboards covered with ivory sugar paste

ivory, pink and lime-green petal paste

small rolling pin

4cm (1⅛in) rose cutter

ball tool

soft foam pad

paintbrush

sugar glue

2.5cm (1in) calyx cutter

25mm (1in) width ivory ribbon for the cakes

royal icing

piping bag

no. 1.5 nozzle

15 silver balls (5mm diameter)

15mm (⅝in) width ivory ribbon to edge baseboards

glue stick

Heart-shaped cakes are very romantic, but they're often considered to be rather old fashioned. For this special cake I have stacked three hearts, surrounded the tiers with a wide satin ribbon and studded the lips of the cake with delicate handmade sugar rosebuds. By adding just a few silver dragées on the sides of the tiers, I have created a clean, modern, stylish cake befitting the most contemporary of occasions.

2 Roll out the green petal paste very thinly. Cut out a calyx shape using a calyx cutter. Use the ball tool and soft pad to gently shape each of the calyx strands. Brush the centre of the calyx with sugar glue and set the rosebud on top. Gently press the calyx into position around the rosebud. For this cake you will need 15 pink rosebuds and 15 ivory ones.

1 To make each rosebud, roll a pea-sized ball of pink petal paste into a cone shape and allow to firm for 1 hour. Roll out a small piece of pink petal paste very thinly and cut out a small rose shape using the cutter. Using a ball tool with a foam pad, gently curve each petal of the rose. Brush a small amount of sugar glue in the centre and place the cone on top. Gently fold a petal up and around the central cone, pinching together the edges to create a sharp point. Push the opposite petal up around the first, then tuck the remaining petals around to create a delicate rosebud. Repeat with ivory petal paste.

To assemble Fix lengths of 25mm (1in) width ivory ribbon around each tier and secure at the back with royal icing. Place the sugar rosebuds on the lips of the cake and baseboards until you are happy with the layout. Pipe a small ball of royal icing onto the base of each one and secure into position. Pipe small balls of icing onto the sides of the cake and top tier only and fix the silver balls in place. Finally, edge the baseboard with the narrow ribbon, securing it in place at the back with glue stick.

daisy chain

you will need

4in round cake covered with marzipan and white sugar paste placed on a 6in round board covered with white sugar paste

rolling pin

55g (2oz) white petal paste

2.5cm (1in) daisy cutter

sharp blade

ball tool

sponge mat

sugar glue

55g (2oz) yellow petal paste

paintbrush

scribe

sugar pollen granules mixed with egg-yellow food colouring

piping bag and no. 2 nozzle

green royal icing

1m (40in) length of wide sheer ribbon

He loves me... He loves me not... He loves me... This design is effective and versatile yet so clean and simple. The daisy heads are made from coloured sugar, then chained together with piped green royal icing. The cake has been finished with a sheer green ribbon. This is also a great design to use on individual cakes.

1 To make the daisies, roll out the white petal paste very thinly. The paste dries out very quickly so only work a few at a time. You will need 2 cut-outs for each daisy. Cut each petal in half using a sharp blade.

2 Using a small ball tool, and with cut-out daisies on a sponge mat, draw petals towards the centre of the daisy. Place one daisy cut-out over another so that the petals overlap. Fix into position with sugar glue.

3 Roll a small piece of yellow petal paste into a dome. Brush with sugar glue, spear on a scribe and dip into yellow pollen granules. Allow to dry.

4 Carefully position the daisy centre inside the flower, securing it in place with sugar glue.

To assemble Pipe a green chain onto the top of the cake and, while it is still wet, press each daisy head into position. Tie the sheer ribbon around the base of the cake.

easter bunny

you will need

8in oval-shaped cake covered with marzipan and mint-green sugar paste

12in oval board covered with mint-green sugar paste and edged with 15mm (⅝in) width mint-green ribbon

2in round individual cakes covered with marzipan and mint-green sugar paste, edged with 15mm (⅝in) width yellow or orange ribbon

200g (7oz) white modelling paste

orange, pink and green food colouring

dried spaghetti

cocktail stick

white and yellow petal paste

ball tool and soft foam pad

sugar glue

paintbrush

white and black royal icing

piping bag

small rolling pin

2.5cm (1in) daffodil cutter

2m (6½ft) length of colourful wired ribbon

This Easter cake is just gorgeous! I wanted to create an oval cake tied with a big, colourful, wired ribbon to create the essence of a giant Easter egg and I have offset the cake on a large oval board, which leaves space to dress it with hand-decorated mini cakes. This idea is great for a party and the little cakes can be presented to each guest or taken home in a gift box.

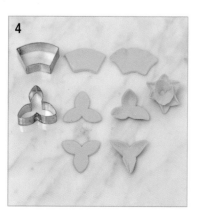

1 Shape the bunny's body and head from white modelling paste as shown. Insert a strand of dried spaghetti to protrude 2.5cm (1in) from the top of the body and use a cocktail stick or the end of a paintbrush to indent the 2 eyes. Make 2 front and 2 back legs and a tail from white petal paste. Make the pieces for the bow tie from orange modelling paste. Prepare a small piece of white modelling paste to resemble the teeth and mark with a cocktail stick. Make 2 jowls from white paste, marking on whiskers with a cocktail stick, and a small triangular nose from pink paste. Make 2 ears from white and pink modelling paste and use a ball tool over a foam pad to gently press the pastes together and bend the ears. Insert a strand of dried spaghetti into each ear to protrude 2cm (¾in).

2 Use sugar glue to assemble the elements of the bunny. Attach the legs and tail to the body as shown, then assemble the bow-tie pieces and fix to the front of the body. Attach the teeth to the head, then fix the jowls into position and add the pink nose. Push the ears into position and pipe eyes with white royal icing followed by black royal icing for the pupils. Carefully position the head onto the body of the bunny.

3 To make each carrot, roll a piece of orange modelling paste into a cone and use a cocktail stick to mark indentations across it. Roll a small cone of green modelling paste to make the carrot top and mark the flat end with a cross. Indent the flat end of the carrot with a cocktail stick and gently push in the green carrot top, securing it with sugar glue.

4 To make each daffodil, roll out a piece of yellow petal paste very thinly and cut out 1 trumpet and 2 sets of petals using a daffodil cutter. Feather the edges of the trumpet and petals with a ball tool. Brush sugar glue in the centre of a petal and place another over the top so petals sit between the ones below. Roll the trumpet into a cylinder and fix into position with sugar glue.

To assemble Place the cake onto the board, offset to one side, and fix it into position with royal icing. Tie wired ribbon around the cake base and finish with a large double bow. Ice the bunny into position on top of the cake and decorate with sugar daffodils and carrots. Secure a carrot or daffodil on the top of each of the mini cakes and set these around the large cake on the board.

summer pavlova

you will need

300g (10½oz) white chocolate

20 small individual meringues and 1 x 8in one (see page 20)

500ml (18fl oz) double cream

250ml (9fl oz) crème pâtissière (or fresh custard sauce)

175g (6oz) ripe mango

1 punnet of fresh raspberries

1 punnet of fresh strawberries

2 punnets of edible flowers

3-tier white chocolate stand – 9in/11in/13in tiers (see page 33)

I designed this cake for a client having an English country wedding in her garden. It was a glorious summer's day. Individual vanilla meringues are pre-lined with white chocolate, filled on site with a mango crème mousseline and topped with fresh seasonal berries and edible flowers. I set them on a white chocolate stand with a larger pavlova on the top for the bride and groom to cut. You may be able to find edible flowers in the herb section of a good supermarket. Alternatively you could ask your local greengrocer to order them especially for you – or even grow your own!

Tip The meringues are filled with fresh cream, which should be kept out of the refrigerator for no longer than 4 hours. Plan your timing carefully as once filled and displayed they should be eaten within 4 hours.

1 Melt the chocolate in a clean bowl in a microwave or over a small saucepan of simmering water. Use a pastry brush to brush the centre of each meringue with melted chocolate. Allow to set.

2 In a large clean bowl whip the cream until it forms soft peaks. Stir in the fresh crème pâtissière. Cut the flesh from the mango and liquidize to make a purée. Stir the mango purée into the cream. Gently crush ½ the raspberries and slice the strawberries and fold into the cream.

3 Place a generous spoonful of the cream carefully on each meringue and fill the large one. Dress with the remainder of the raspberries and finish with an edible flower on each pavlova.

To assemble Carefully set the pavlova on the white chocolate stand, starting with the base tier and working upwards. Place the larger pavlova on the top.

winter pavlova

you will need

400g (14oz) dark chocolate

36 individual hazelnut meringues (see page 20)

3 x 400g (14oz) cans apricots in syrup

900ml (30fl oz) double cream

18 cape gooseberries

20 piped chocolate decorations (see page 70)

zest and juice of 3 unwaxed medium lemons

4-tier dark chocolate stand (see page 33)

This is an adaptation of a delicious hazelnut meringue gâteau my Mother used to make when I was a child. Apricots have an amazing affinity with hazelnut meringue and each is served here with a delicious apricot coulis. To toast the hazelnuts, place them on a baking sheet and bake in the centre of the oven for 15–20 minutes or until deep golden brown, then rub off the skins and finely chop the nuts.

1 Melt the chocolate in a clean bowl in a microwave or over a small saucepan of simmering water. Use a pastry brush to brush the centre of each meringue with melted chocolate. Allow to set.

2 Drain the apricots, reserving the syrup for the coulis. Liquidize the apricots to make a purée. In a large clean bowl, whip the cream until it gently forms soft peaks. Carefully fold 6 rounded tablespoons of apricot purée into the cream. Place a generous spoonful of the cream onto each meringue. Dress some with a single cape gooseberry and others with a chocolate decoration.

3 To make the coulis, add reserved apricot syrup to the remaining apricot purée. Add lemon zest and juice to the sauce, stir well and chill. Serve with the meringues.

To assemble Carefully set the filled meringues on the dark chocolate stand, starting with the base tier and working upwards one tier at a time.

chocolate bonfire

you will need

10in single-layer square chocolate truffle torte layered with chocolate ganache buttercream

4 cutters – 5cm/7.5cm/10cm/12.5cm (2in/3in/4in/5in)

6in round board

1 quantity of chocolate ganache buttercream

500g (1lb 2oz) dark chocolate plastique

rolling pin

icing sugar

sharp knife

ruby, gold, sapphire and copper lustres

edible varnish (optional)

500g (1lb 2oz) fresh autumnal berries and fruit (raspberries, grapes, blackberries, blueberries, cape gooseberries, cherries)

indoor sparklers to decorate (optional)

Ideal Hallowe'en food – rich layers of chocolate torte with lashings of chocolate ganache buttercream, wrapped up in dark chocolate and set alight with fireworks. I have lustered the chocolate with fiery colours and dressed the cake with autumnal berries. This cake is a smaller version of the white helter-skelter with strawberries (see page 137) and as such is constructed entirely from cake without the need for a polystyrene cone.

1 Using the 4 different sizes of cutter, cut out 4 rounds of cake from the single-tier chocolate torte. Place the largest round on the 6in round board. Use chocolate ganache buttercream to stack the cakes together and cover the sides.

2 Knead the dark chocolate plastique until smooth and pliable. Divide into 2 and roll one half on a work surface lightly dusted with icing sugar into a long strip approximately 46 x 10cm (18 x 4in). Use a sharp knife to neaten both long edges, then, with the end of a rolling pin, feather one of the long edges (see page 137). Beginning at the bottom

of the cake and with the straight edge of the chocolate plastique strip flush with the base of the cake, carefully wrap the chocolate around the cake as shown.

3 Repeat with the next piece of chocolate plastique, creating interesting pockets and shapes as you work upwards, finishing with a flourish. Gild the chocolate with strong fiery lustres and spray with edible varnish if desired. Just before serving, dress the cake with fresh berries, placing them in the pockets created by the chocolate plastique covering. Push indoor sparklers into the cake, if desired.

hallowe'en cookies

The ideal trick or treat gift – handmade spiced cookies in the shape of bats and pumpkins are decorated with sugar paste and coloured royal icing. These cookies are fun to make with children, who can create the scariest or happiest pumpkin faces.

amaryllis christmas

you will need

8in round cake covered with marzipan and white sugar paste

11in round board covered with white sugar paste

200g (7oz) white petal paste

old-gold edible food colouring

small rolling pin

paintbrush

gold lustre

10cm (4in) holly cutter

marking tool or cocktail stick

sponge

1.35m (5½ft) length of 15mm (⅝in) width gold ribbon (for ribbon loops)

2.7m (11ft) length of 15mm (⅝in) width white ribbon (for ribbon loops)

26-gauge white and green florist's wires, cut into 10cm (4in) lengths

white and green florist's tape

21 large white stamens

small veining rolling pin

7.5cm (3in) amaryllis cutter

10cm (4in) amaryllis veining mould

ball tool and soft foam pad

green dusting powder

piping bag filled with white royal icing

75cm (2½ft) length of 25mm (1in) width white ribbon and 75cm (2½ft) length of 15mm (⅝in) width gold ribbon (for the cake)

glue stick

1m (3ft) length of 15mm (⅝in) width white ribbon (for the board)

1cm (½in) diameter posy pick

White amaryllis are one of my favourite flowers and, as they are available in the winter, are a natural choice for this luxurious gold and white Christmas cake. This would make a perfect design for a special wedding anniversary celebrated at this time of year: simply change the colour of the ribbon – gold for 50 years, ruby for 40 years or silver for 25 years.

1 Knead petal paste until soft and pliable. Reserve half for the amaryllis petals and colour half the remainder old gold. Roll out thinly using a small rolling pin. Use a paintbrush to cover with gold lustre. Cut out 4 holly leaves and score veins with a marking tool. Arrange leaves on the cake. Make 4 white leaves with white petal paste and position them between the gold ones. Use pieces of sponge to hold leaves in place and leave to dry.

2 Cut gold ribbon into 3 lengths of 15cm (6in) and 3 lengths of 30cm (12in). Cut white ribbon into 6 lengths of 15cm (6in) and 6 lengths of 30cm (12in). Fold one end of a long length of ribbon over to create a loop with a tail approximately 10cm (4in) long. Hold one of the short lengths against the other side of the loop.

3 Hold the ends of the loops against a white florist's wire. Secure in place with white florist's tape, winding it all the way to the bottom of the wire. Repeat with the other ribbons.

4 Tape together a length of green florist's wire with 7 stamens using florist's tape. As the tape is pulled taut it becomes self-adhesive. Wrap the tape around the stamens all the way to the end of the wire for stability. Repeat twice more (you will need one for each amaryllis flower).

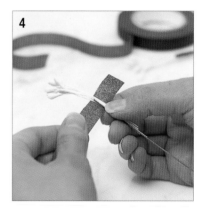

5 Prepare 6 amaryllis petals for each flower. Using the veining rolling pin, thinly roll out the remaining white petal paste. Place the amaryllis cutter on the paste with the thick vein in the centre and cut out 6 petals. Insert approximately 2cm (¾in) of a length of white florist's wire into the thick vein as shown. Lay the wired petal inside the veining mould with the wire facing outwards and firmly press the mould sides together to indent the markings on the petal. Use a ball tool over a foam pad to gently feather the edges of the petal. Allow the petals to dry overnight propped over an upturned bowl or cylindrical tube so that they gently curve backwards.

6 Paint the centre length of each petal with green dusting powder.

7 Tape the first 3 petals evenly around the central stamens using florist's tape. Add the final 3 petals one at a time and secure with florist's tape. Finally, tape 1 gold and 2 white ribbon loops at even intervals around each of the finished amaryllis using green florist's tape.

To assemble Fill a small piping bag with white royal icing and snip the top with sharp scissors. Fix the wide white ribbon around the cake and overlay it with the thin gold ribbon, securing both at the back with royal icing. Glue the thin white ribbon around the baseboard. Remove the sponge from the leaves and secure them into position on the cake with icing. Push the posy pick into the centre of the cake until it is flush with the top. Pipe royal icing into the posy pick and gently insert the 3 amaryllis and ribbon loops. Trim the ribbon ends as necessary.

Tip These sugar paste amaryllis are extremely fragile! Handle the petals at the base where the wire is inserted as this is the most stable point and prepare extra petals for each flower – if one snaps it can be pulled out and another taped into position.

christmas tree

you will need

8in oval cake covered with marzipan and purple sugar paste

100g (3½oz) white sugar paste

100g (3½oz) white petal paste

rolling pin

3 star cutters – 2.5cm/5cm/7.5cm (1in/2in/3in)

55g (2oz) white royal icing

piping bag

silver dragées

1m (40in) length of star ribbon

For a more contemporary Christmas cake, I have covered this oval-shaped cake with a regal purple sugar paste. The white Christmas tree is made from a stack of white stars in different sizes studded with silver dragées. To complement the cake I have used a white star ribbon.

Tip Using an equal mixture of sugar paste and petal paste to make the stars for the Christmas tree gives the finished tree strength and allows it to set firmly more quickly.

1 Combine the sugar paste and petal paste together and knead until smooth and pliable. Roll out to a thickness of 4mm (⅛in). Cut out 2 or 3 stars of each size.

2 Starting with the largest stars, pipe a small amount of royal icing in the centre of each and stack the next one on top at a slight angle. Repeat until the tree is approximately 15cm (6in) high, using 8–10 stars.

To assemble Place the final star upright on top of the tree as shown. Fix the tree into position on the top of the cake and add silver dragées using royal icing. Tie the star ribbon around the cake.

individual christmas cakes

you will need

5cm (2in) round cakes covered with marzipan and white sugar paste

green, red and white petal paste

rolling pin

white royal icing

templates (see page 150), optional

tracing paper (optional)

scribe

piping bags

no. 1.5, no. 2 and no. 5 nozzles

red, brown, black, yellow, ivory and peach edible food colours

holly cutter

Christmas tree cutter

paintbrush

gold lustre

alcohol dipping solution

6mm (¼in) width red ribbon to fix around the base of each cake

These adorable individual Christmas cakes are such fun to make and they make the most wonderful stocking fillers. I have also used them, presented in clear boxes tied with a ribbon, as place settings for the Christmas table. Although I have provided a template for the angel and reindeer, try piping these freehand once you have built up confidence so each character is unique.

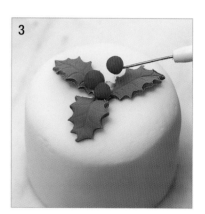

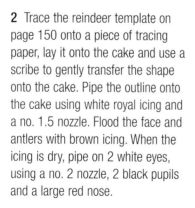

1 To make the Santa hat, form a piece of red petal paste into a cone and fold the top over gently. Roll out a ball of white petal paste and gently press this between your thumb and forefinger to create a flattened disk. Press the red cone onto the white base. Cut the hat in half vertically and ice into position on the cake. Make a white ball of petal paste for the bobble and fix into position.

2 Trace the reindeer template on page 150 onto a piece of tracing paper, lay it onto the cake and use a scribe to gently transfer the shape onto the cake. Pipe the outline onto the cake using white royal icing and a no. 1.5 nozzle. Flood the face and antlers with brown icing. When the icing is dry, pipe on 2 white eyes, using a no. 2 nozzle, 2 black pupils and a large red nose.

3 To make the holly and berries, roll out the green petal paste very thinly and cut out 3 holly leaves. Curl the leaves very gently and ice them into position on the cake. Roll a piece of red petal paste into 3 small balls to make the berries and fix these into position with royal icing.

4 For the Christmas tree, roll out the green petal paste very thinly and cut out a Christmas tree shape. Ice into position on the cake. Pipe a white star on the top of the tree using a no. 5 nozzle and 5 red baubles using a no. 1.5 nozzle.

5 Transfer the angel template on page 150 onto the cake. Pipe around the outline of the shape using white royal icing and a no. 1.5 nozzle. Mix a small amount of ivory and peach coloured icing together to create a skin colour and use to flood the face and feet. Flood the hair and pipe a halo in golden yellow and flood the wings white. Allow to dry, then using a paintbrush and food colour, add the facial details. Lustre the hair and halo with gold lustre powder. Finally, fix a length of ribbon around the base of each cake, securing it at the back with royal icing.

christmas parcel

you will need

2 x 6in square cakes stacked together with apricot jam or buttercream

pastry brush

apricot jam

1.75kg (3lb 14oz) marzipan

brandy

2.25kg (5lb) red sugar paste

icing sugar

rolling pin

ruler

sharp knife

18cm (7in) square piece of paper

100g (3½oz) white sugar paste

4cm (1½in) star cutter

greaseproof paper

sugar glue

edible glitter

2.5m (8ft) length of colourful wired ribbon

royal icing

9in square board covered with red sugar paste and edged with 1m (40in) length of 15mm (⅝in) wide red ribbon

This cake has been made to look like a tantalizing Christmas present box. It is a versatile design that can be adapted for many occasions by changing the colours and ribbon. The cake is very deep, made up of two 6in square cakes to form a cube.

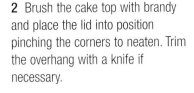

1 Brush the cake with boiled apricot jam and cover with marzipan in panels as though it were to be covered with royal icing. (This will give the box squarer edges.) Brush the top and sides of the cake with brandy. Knead the red sugar paste until smooth and pliable and divide into 3 equal portions. Lightly dust a work surface with icing sugar and roll out two-thirds of the sugar paste into a large rectangle. Use a ruler and cut a fat strip large enough to fit around the 4 sides of the box in one piece. Use a knife to trim the icing so it is flush with the top of the cake. Roll out the remaining one-third of the sugar paste and cut out a 25cm (10in) square. Lay an 18cm (7in) square piece of paper in the centre (to allow for depth of marzipan and icing) and trim away the 4 corners as shown to form the box lid.

2 Brush the cake top with brandy and place the lid into position pinching the corners to neaten. Trim the overhang with a knife if necessary.

3 Knead the white sugar paste until smooth and pliable. Lightly dust a work surface with icing sugar and roll out the paste to a thickness of 4mm (⅛in). Cut out several white stars and allow to dry.

4 Place the stars onto a clean sheet of greaseproof paper. Brush with sugar glue and pour edible glitter over the top.

5 Cut the wired ribbon in half. Lay the 2 pieces across one another to form a large cross. Sit the cake centrally on top. Draw the 4 edges of the ribbon up and tie into a bow on the top. Fix the stars into position on the cake with royal icing. Fix the cake into position on the iced board.

Tip This cake works as a maximum 15cm- (6in-) height box. Any deeper and the cake will be too heavy to support itself. If you want to make the cake larger, use a larger square tin, but keep to this height.

winter igloo

you will need

10in round cake covered with marzipan and white sugar paste

5in dome cake (use one half of a ball sphere tin) covered with marzipan and white sugar paste

16in round board covered with white sugar paste

marking tool

white, black, red, blue and orange modelling paste

paintbrush

sugar glue

piping bags

no. 1.5 and no. 2 nozzles

white and black royal icing

piping gel

1m (3ft) length of 25mm (1in) width white ribbon for the cake

1m (3ft) length of 15mm (⅝in) width light blue ribbon for the cake

white hologram edible glitter

1.5m (5ft) length of 15mm (⅝in) width white ribbon to edge the baseboard

glue stick (to fix ribbon around baseboard)

This cake was originally designed for a very special girl's third birthday. The cute polar bears and penguins are made from modelling paste, although the igloo is a real cake. Why not make the base cake one flavour and have the igloo as another flavour – just for the birthday person? Dust the snowballs with glitter and the tongues and noses of the polar bears with piping gel for authenticity.

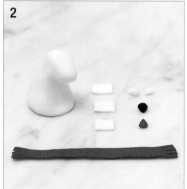

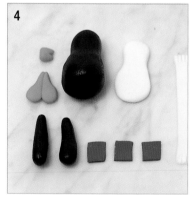

1 With a marking tool score concentric circles around the igloo working upwards. Mark vertical lines to represent bricks. Make the entrance of the igloo from a sausage of white modelling paste, slightly hollowed out at one end, and square the sides gently. Score the bricks using the marking tool.

2 Mould modelling paste into the various parts of the polar bear as shown: white for the polar bear's body and ears and squares for the scarf; red for the scarf and tongue and black for the nose.

3 Attach the ears, nose and tongue onto the head, and squares onto the scarf, with sugar glue. Brush the back of the scarf with sugar glue and wrap around the polar bear. Pipe eyes using white royal icing with a no. 2 nozzle, followed by a black pupil with a no. 1.5 nozzle. Brush the nose and tongue with piping gel to create a glistening wet effect.

4 To make the penguin, mould black modelling paste into body shape and 2 wings. Use white paste to make the front of the body and a scarf, orange for the feet and beak and blue for the squares on scarf.

5 Use sugar glue to fix the front of the body onto the black body shape and to attach wings to shoulders. Flatten the ends of the wings so they sit away from the body. Fix feet, beak and scarf in position with sugar glue. Use black royal icing and a no. 2 nozzle to pipe 2 eyes.

To assemble Offset the cake on the lined board and fix the wider white ribbon, overlaid with the blue ribbon, around it. Secure the igloo, igloo entrance, penguins and polar bears in position on top of the cake with royal icing. Make snowballs from white modelling paste and ice them into place on the cake. Brush them with sugar glue then with white hologram glitter. Use the narrower white ribbon to edge the baseboard.

building blocks

you will need

25 x 5cm (2in) cake cubes, covered with marzipan and white, pink or blue sugar paste

pink and blue sugar paste for polka dots

sugar glue

paintbrush

white sugar rosebuds (see page 87)

white royal icing

piping bag

no. 1.5 and no. 3 piping nozzles

12mm (½in) width white, pink and blue ribbon

white, light blue, dark blue, light brown, dark brown and pink modelling paste

dried spaghetti

star-marking tool

brown liquid food colouring

4-tier iced stand – 8in/10in/12in/14in boards edged with 15mm (⅝in) width ribbon and polystyrene blocks wrapped with 25mm (1in) width ribbon

1cm (½in) cubes of sugar paste

Individual building-block cakes are a lovely idea for a child's christening or first birthday. I have made this cake in shades of blue and pink with a model of a teddy bear and his train on the top – change the colour of the sugar paste on the cakes or mould another sugar toy on the top to personalize the design. The little building blocks are made from coloured sugar paste and are presented on a purpose-built stand, adding height and drama to the cake.

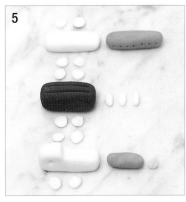

1 Cover some of the white cakes with polka dots made from tiny flattened balls of pink or blue sugar paste fixed in position on the cakes with sugar glue.

2 Attach a white sugar rosebud (see page 87) to each of the remaining white cakes using royal icing. Pipe letters or numbers onto the pink and blue cakes using the no. 3 nozzle. Fix ribbon around the base of each cake, holding it in position at the back with royal icing.

3 Shape a body for the teddy bear from white modelling paste and insert a strand of dried spaghetti to protrude from the top. Mark stars on the body using the star-marking tool. Following the picture, make arms, slippers and a hat from dark blue paste; collar, cuffs, hat brim and pompom from pale blue paste; head, ear, hands and feet from dark brown paste and a face from the light brown paste.

4 Using sugar glue, attach arms, cuffs, hands, feet and shoes to the body, and ear and face to the head. Thread the collar onto the body, then secure the head. Attach the brim and pompom to the hat. Insert a strand of spaghetti into the head to support the hat and thread it on. Paint eyes, nose and mouth with brown food colour.

5 Make 12 train wheels from white modelling paste and mould white, blue and pink blocks as shown. Fix all pieces together with sugar glue to form the engine and 2 carriages.

To assemble Position the individual cakes onto the stand starting with the base tier and working upwards. Fill a piping bag with a no. 1.5 nozzle and fresh white royal icing and ice the teddy bear into position on the top board together with the train set and 1cm (½in) cubes of sugar paste to resemble building blocks.

birthday clown

you will need

8in oval-shaped cake covered with marzipan and purple sugar paste

11in oval board covered with purple sugar paste

2m (6½ft) length of colourful wired ribbon to tie around the cake

template (see page 150)

tracing paper

waxed paper

masking tape

piping bags

no 1.5 nozzle

150g (5½oz) white royal icing

red, yellow, blue, green and black edible food colours

paintbrush

yellow, green and blue sugar paste

star cutter

1m (40in) length of 15mm (⅝in) width purple ribbon to fix around the board

glue stick (to fix ribbon around board)

chocolate drops (optional)

Children's birthday parties tend to conjure up images of painted faces, party games, balloons, streamers, toys and a special birthday cake. It is becoming common for children to have themed parties, sometimes with professional entertainers, and clowns are a particularly popular choice. This cake would complement such an occasion very well. I have added some brightly coloured chocolate drops around the cake for those too impatient to wait until the candles have been blown out!

1 Position the cake centrally onto the board. Fix the ribbon around the base of the cake and tie with a bow. Transfer the template on page 150 onto tracing paper. On a flat work surface, fix a sheet of waxed paper over the design and secure with masking tape. Fill a piping bag with a no. 1.5 nozzle and white royal icing and pipe around the clown template as shown. Do not pipe the balloon strings or the clown's facial features.

2 Place 1 tablespoon of royal icing into each of 4 bowls and thin with a little water to create flooding icing. Colour the icing in one bowl red, one yellow, one green and one blue. Fill a piping bag with red flooding icing, snip the end and flood the clown's body. Before it has had time to set, fill a second piping bag with a

no. 1.5 nozzle and yellow flooding icing and drop yellow spots into position using a paintbrush so they merge into the red. Continue to flood sections of the clown, allowing time for the icing to form a crust before flooding adjoining sections. Allow to dry overnight. Pipe the facial features and black detail with royal icing.

To assemble Carefully peel the waxed paper away from the clown and fix the clown into position on the cake with royal icing. Pipe the balloon strings using black royal icing. Roll out the coloured sugar paste and stamp out several stars. Fix these into position on the cake and board. Edge the board with narrow ribbon and, if you wish, dress the table with hand-decorated chocolate drops.

teddy bear christening

you will need

8in petal-shaped cake covered with marzipan and yellow sugar paste

3 petal-shaped boards – 8in/11in/12in, largest only covered with yellow sugar paste

scribe

100g (3½oz) white royal icing

2 piping bags

no. 1.5 and no. 3 nozzles

250g (9oz) white modelling paste

light brown, dark brown and yellow edible food colouring

dried spaghetti

marking tools

small rolling pin

flower stamps (small and medium)

sugar glue

55g (2oz) royal icing – white and black

1.5m (4ft) length of 15mm (⅝in) width white ribbon to fix around 12in baseboard

glue stick (to fix ribbon around board)

One of the very first cakes I made was a christening cake for my god-daughter Hannah. It, too, was a delicate petal-shaped cake dressed with yellow and white. Here I have added a pretty 'needlepoint' design around the top edge of the cake, which is mirrored around the board. The cake is finished with a plump sugar teddy bear holding a building block.

1 Place the 11in board centrally over the 12in covered board and scribe around the outside. Position the cake centrally onto the covered board and fix into position with royal icing. Place the 8in board centrally over the cake and scribe around the outside. Using a no. 3 nozzle and fresh white royal icing, pipe a trail of pearls around the base of the cake. Using a no. 1.5 nozzle, pipe the picot and heart design around the top of the cake and the cake board as shown. Keep the 2 lobes of the heart and the double picot pearls on the scribed line as you work around.

2 To make the teddy bear, divide the modelling paste into 5 equal balls and colour 2 light brown, 1 dark brown and 1 yellow. With the light brown paste make the body, arms, feet and circles for the face. Insert a piece of dried spaghetti so it protrudes 2.5cm (1in) out of the top of the body. Make the ribbons, bow and small building block with the yellow modelling paste; the head, ears and nose from dark brown paste; and the dress from white paste, as shown. Roll out a small amount of paste thinly and stamp out 16–18 yellow or white small flowers.

3 Place the dress over the body and gently fold the base to create movement. Attach all elements of the body and clothes as shown, using sugar glue. Use royal icing to pipe the eyes and fix the small flowers into position around the top edge of the teddy's dress and by one ear. Pipe a letter on the building block and pipe the centres of all the flowers.

To assemble Fix the teddy bear on the cake with royal icing and add a few cut-out flowers in various colours and sizes. Pipe the 'AaBbCc' on the cake and attach ribbon to the board.

AaBbCc

easter cookies

These cute Easter cookies – chicks, butterflies and flowers – are brightly decorated with sugar paste and royal icing. They make lovely gifts presented in a clear bag tied with a pretty ribbon.

christmas cookies

Christmas is a time for giving and these hand-decorated spiced cookies make wonderful gifts presented in clear cellophane bags or gift boxes tied with a red ribbon. Alternatively, make a hole in the top of the cookies with a straw before they are baked and hang the decorated cookies with ribbon on your Christmas tree. These cookies are fun to make with children and make great presents for grandparents and school teachers.

1 Stamp out shapes from a batch of cookie dough using cutters in Christmas shapes – reindeers, Christmas trees, holly, stars and angels. Bake the cookies following the instructions on page 21. Colour some sugar paste brown for reindeers and green for trees and holly, leaving some white for stars and angels. Knead the sugar paste until smooth and pliable and roll out to 3mm (⅛in) thick on a work surface lightly dusted with icing sugar. Use the cookie cutter to cut out the sugar paste and fix it into position on the cookie with royal icing.

2 Use coloured royal icing to pipe decorations onto the sugar paste-topped cookies. For the reindeers, pipe black antlers, a white eye and black pupil, and a large red nose.

3 Christmas trees can be decorated with red 'baubles' and a white star, using a star nozzle. Allow the cookies to dry before wrapping them in clear cellophane bags and tying with ribbon. The cookies will remain fresh for 7 days if kept in an airtight container.

signature cakes

signature style

The cakes in this section are all firm favourites from my personal portfolio. Each has been inspired, designed and created to reflect my clean, classical, contemporary style. I have been allowed to indulge my passion here and present a collection of beautifully romantic, flawless jewels with exceptional attention to detail. Several of these designs are based on exquisite jewellery, including the Fabergé and black-pearl tiara. You could personalize your own cake by adapting the design of a family heirloom, tiara, necklace or brooch. Many of these cakes can be adapted in size, shape and colour to complement your special occasion so you may create your own spectacular cake.

1950s chic

you will need

3-tier square cake – 4in/6in/8in tiers covered with marzipan and white royal icing, placed on boards 3in larger than each tier covered with white royal icing

piping bag

no. 3 nozzle

200g (7oz) white royal icing

2 polystyrene blocks (10cm/4in smaller than the middle and base tiers)

fresh, wired flowers to dress

8 dowels

1.5m (5ft) length of 15mm (⅝in) width white ribbon to edge the boards

glue stick (to fix ribbon around boards)

This 1950s chic design – one of my favourite wedding cakes – was inspired by style icons of an era that has popular appeal today. The square tiers are royal iced to achieve clean sharp edges that are then hand piped with a pinstripe design in white royal icing. I have finished each tier with a row of royal-iced pearls around the top and base edge then blocked the wedding cake with fresh white roses and paper white narcissi.

Fill a piping bag with no. 3 nozzle and white royal icing and pipe vertical lines at equal distances around each tier. Pipe a trail of pearls around the top and base edge of each tier and allow to dry.

To assemble Stud the polystyrene blocks with fresh, wired flowers (see page 53). Stack the tiers by inserting dowels (with a gentle boring motion to avoid cracking the icing), following instructions on page 34. Finally, edge the boards with white ribbon.

cascading lily

you will need

3-tier round cake – 6in/9in/12in tiers covered with marzipan and white sugar paste and stacked centrally on 16in round board covered with white sugar paste

24-gauge wires, each cut into 3 equal lengths

white petal paste

paintbrush

green dusting powder

large white lily stamens

green florist's tape

small veining rolling pin

10cm (4in) lily cutter

26-gauge wires, each cut into 3 equal lengths

10cm (4in) lily-veining mould

ball tool

soft foam pad

pink dusting powder

brown liquid food colouring

2.5m (8ft) length of 12mm (½in) width ivory ribbon

1.5m (5ft) length of 15mm (⅝in) width ivory ribbon

150g (5½oz) white royal icing

piping bag and no. 3 nozzle

12 posy picks

white wire curls made with 28-gauge wire

Tip You will need 6 petals for each lily but as they're very fragile, it is a good idea to make extra. If a petal snaps, pull it out gently and tape another into position.

I like the fresh, clean feel of this stacked cake, which has been decorated with hand-piped cascading pearls and dressed with handmade sugar lilies. The wire curls are made by twisting a length of 28-gauge wire around a single dowel. By changing the colours of the lilies this cake can be adapted to complement your wedding, or can be used for a single-tier anniversary cake.

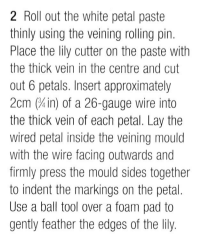

1 Bend the top of a 24-gauge wire over to form a small hook. Form white petal paste into an elongated cone, pinch the blunt end into 3 and mark with a cross. Insert the hooked end of the wire gently into the thin end of the cone and allow to dry overnight before brushing with green dusting powder. Position 6 large lily stamens around the centre and tape into position with green florist's tape.

2 Roll out the white petal paste thinly using the veining rolling pin. Place the lily cutter on the paste with the thick vein in the centre and cut out 6 petals. Insert approximately 2cm (¾in) of a 26-gauge wire into the thick vein of each petal. Lay the wired petal inside the veining mould with the wire facing outwards and firmly press the mould sides together to indent the markings on the petal. Use a ball tool over a foam pad to gently feather the edges of the lily.

3 Allow the lily petals to dry overnight propped over an upturned bowl so that the petals gently curve backwards. (For a more closed lily dry the petals flat.) Dust the centre length of each petal with pink dusting powder and use a paintbrush dipped into brown liquid food colouring to paint small dots on top. Allow to dry.

4 Tape the first 3 petals evenly around the central stamens using florist's tape. Add the final 3 petals one at a time and fix in position with tape. Handle the lilies at the base where the wire is inserted as this is the most stable point.

To assemble Secure lengths of narrower ribbon around each tier and wider ribbon round the baseboard, fixing at the back with royal icing. Starting with the top tier and working downwards, pipe random pearls, concentrating them at the base of each tier, as shown. Use a clean paintbrush to remove the point of each pearl and leave the cake to dry overnight. Push the posy picks into the cake at intervals, fill them with royal icing and insert the sugar flowers and wire curls into each.

corsage rose

you will need

8in round cake covered with marzipan and sugar paste and placed offset onto a 12in board covered with sugar paste

24-gauge wires

green florist's tape

deep red petal paste

small rolling pin

3 rose cutters – 4cm/5cm/7.5cm (1½in/2in/3in)

ball tool

soft foam pad

paintbrush

sugar glue

pale pink petal paste

forest-green petal paste

6.5cm (2½in) calyx cutter

2 rose-leaf cutters – 4cm/5cm (1½in/2in)

1m (3ft) length of 32mm (1¼in) width fuchsia-pink ribbon

2m (6½ft) length of 15mm (⅝in) width red ribbon

piping bag and no.1.5 nozzle

55g (2oz) royal icing

50 silver ball dragées (0.5mm diameter)

2m (6½ft) total length of 12mm (½in) width ribbon in shades of red and pink made into 5 triple ribbon bows

5 green wire curls made with 28-gauge wire (see page 121)

2 posy picks

This vintage cake design was originally commissioned by *Vogue* magazine after I had designed the wedding cake for Madonna and Guy Ritchie. Inspired by blousy corsage fabric roses, it is dressed with handmade oversized sugar roses. Although I have chosen here to decorate a single tier, this design transposes well for an elegant wedding cake. Make roses in shades of antique ivory and caramel and use them to decorate a tiered, stacked, royal-iced cake.

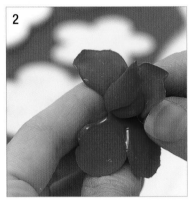

1 Cut one 24-gauge wire into 4 equal lengths and tape them together using florist's tape. Bend the top 3mm (⅛in) over to create a hook. Taper a cone shape of hazelnut-sized red petal paste onto the hooked wire. Allow to dry and firm overnight.

2 Roll out a small piece of red petal paste and cut out a small rose shape. Use a ball tool over a foam pad to gently curve each petal. Brush a small amount of sugar glue in the centre of the rose and thread the wire through the centre. Gently fold petals up and around the cone to create a delicate rose bud. Allow to set overnight. Repeat to make 2 roses with the 5cm (2in) cutter and 2 with the 7.5cm (3in) cutter, some from pink petal paste.

3 Roll out the green paste very thinly and cut out a calyx shape using a 6.5cm (2½in) calyx cutter. Use the ball tool over a soft pad to gently shape each of the calyx strands. Brush the calyx with sugar glue and thread the rose onto the calyx. Gently press a small cone of green paste into position for stability. Make leaves from green petal paste following the instructions for making lily petals on page 121.

To assemble Fix the wide fuchsia ribbon around the cake and overlay it with the narrower red ribbon. Edge the board with red ribbon. Using a piping bag with a no. 1.5 nozzle and white royal icing, attach the silver balls randomly around the cake. Arrange together a selection of roses, leaves, ribbon loops and wire curls using florist's tape. Insert the posy picks into the cake, fill with icing and insert the flower sprays.

butterflies

you will need

4-tier round cake – 4in/6in/8in/10in tiers covered with white sugar paste, stacked centrally and placed on 13in and 16in boards covered with white sugar paste

7m (23ft) length of 15mm (⅝in) width white ribbon

butterfly template (see page 151)

tracing paper

waxed paper

masking tape

piping bags

no. 1.5 and no. 3 nozzles

500g (1lb 2oz) white royal icing (yields 16–20 butterflies)

buttercup yellow and leaf green food colours

paintbrush

cocktail stick

sponge cut into 1cm (⅜in) cubes (or cotton wool)

20 flower stamens, cut in half

55g (2oz) petal paste

2.5cm (1in) calyx cutter

ball tool and foam pad

These delicate sugar butterflies epitomize summer without the use of flowers. Made from royal icing in a run-out technique, they can be a mass of bright colours or in soft pastels. They can be used to dress wedding, birthday or christening cakes or iced into position on individual cakes. Little cakes can be presented in a clear box finished with a ribbon for guests to take home as favours.

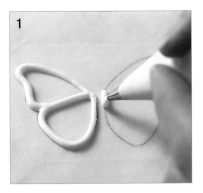

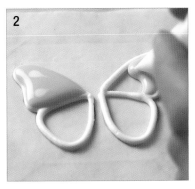

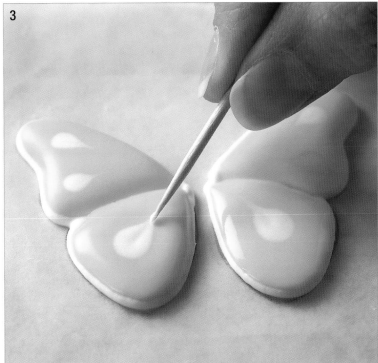

1 Fix lengths of ribbon around each tier and around the baseboards. Trace a selection of butterfly designs (see page 151) onto tracing paper and fix a piece of waxed paper over the top, shiny side up, holding both in position with masking tape. Using a no. 1.5 nozzle and white royal icing, pipe the outline.

2 Reserve 2 large tablespoons of royal icing and thin remainder with water as flooding icing. Separate into 3 bowls, colour one yellow and one green. Fill 3 piping bags with icing and flood the butterflies. Use a small damp paintbrush to pull the icing to fill all the corners.

3 While the icing is still wet, add detail with the other colours inside the wings and drag with a cocktail stick to form patterns. Allow to set for 15 minutes then flood the lower wings. Leave the iced butterfy wings overnight to dry .

4 Peel the butterfly wings from the waxed paper. Fill a piping bag with a no. 3 nozzle and reserved royal icing. Pipe a head and body onto clean waxed paper and then attach wings onto the iced body at an angle, supporting each one with a small piece of sponge (or cotton wool). Insert 2 stamens for antennae. Leave to dry overnight.

To assemble Cut out tiny flowers from white petal paste using a calyx cutter. Form with a ball tool over a foam pad. Allow to dry. Fix butterflies and flowers onto the cake with icing. Pipe flower centres with yellow icing.

fleur-de-lis

you will need

4-tier round cake – 6in/8in/10in/12in tiers covered with marzipan and ivory sugar paste

15in round board covered with ivory sugar paste

template (see page 151)

greaseproof paper

pen

masking tape

scribe

piping bag fitted with a no. 2 nozzle

200g (7oz) white royal icing

topaz lustre

edible gel

paintbrush

3m (10ft) length of 12mm (½in) width ivory ribbon to fix around the base of each tier

1.5m (5ft) length of 15mm (⅝in) width ivory ribbon for the board

This is a smaller replica of the six-tier wedding cake I created for Pierce Brosnan and Keely Shaye Smith. The tiers are stacked and I have dressed the cake here with fresh apricot amaryllis and delicate white sweet peas. The design is repeated three times symmetrically around each tier. As the circumference will change for every cake it is impossible to provide one definitive template. Follow the instructions given on page 151 to ensure that the design lines up perfectly on each tier.

1 Transfer the template on page 151 onto greaseproof paper and fix around the cake, holding in position with masking tape. Use a scribe to prick the design onto the cake.

2 Fill a piping bag with a no.2 nozzle and white royal icing. Pipe the design as shown, including all the pearls. Allow to dry. Blend ½ teaspoon of topaz lustre with 1 teaspoon edible gel and glaze each pearl using a paintbrush.

To assemble Allow each tier to dry before stacking the tiers centrally. Finish by wrapping the narrower ribbon around the base of each tier and the wider ribbon around the baseboard, securing it at the back of the cake with royal icing.

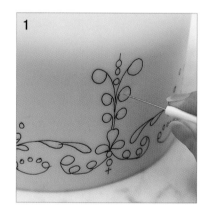

contemporary romantic

I find the clean, simple lines of this contemporary cake aesthetically pleasing and it has proved to be a firm favourite with many others too. After it was featured in a bridal magazine in the UK, I received more calls than I have for any other cake. However, because it is so simple, it needs to be precision perfect with hidden construction.

you will need

4-tier square cake – 6in/8in/10in/12in tiers placed on boards the same size and covered (to the base of each board) with marzipan and ivory sugar paste

4 boards, 3in larger than each cake tier (for transporting the cakes only)

3 square 5cm- (2in-) deep polystyrene blocks – 10cm/13cm/15cm (4in/5in/6in)

12 dowels

60 fresh, wired roses ('Blue Curioso') to dress

palette knife

Carefully set the tiers down onto plain boards 3in larger to dry and allow for transportation. Position the polystyrene blocks and insert the dowels (see page 34). Block each tier with fresh, wired roses (see page 53) before you attempt to assemble the cake.

To assemble Because the tiers are on hidden boards, you'll need to handle the cakes with extreme care to avoid damaging the icing around the base. Gently move the cake to the edge of the protective board using a palette knife to loosen the cake and allow you to grasp it from underneath. Repeat with other tiers.

aroma romantic

This is an adaptation of the contemporary romantic wedding cake shown opposite. I have added a wide ribbon around the base of a two-tier hexagonal cake, which can mask an unsightly edge, and have finished the cake by randomly hand piping tiny pearls on each tier. The cake has been blocked with fresh aromatic roses.

you will need

2-tier hexagonal cake – 9in/12in tiers placed on boards the same size and covered (to the base of each board) with marzipan and ivory sugar paste

2 boards, 3in larger than cake tiers (for transporting the cakes only)

2m (6½ft) length of 25mm (1in) width ivory satin ribbon

55g (2oz) royal icing

piping bag

no. 1.5 nozzle

4 dowels

12.5cm (5in) round x 5cm (2in) depth polystyrene block

20 fresh, wired roses ('Aroma') to dress

Carefully set the tiers down onto plain boards 3in larger to dry and allow for transportation. Fix lengths of ribbon around the base of each tier and fix in position with royal icing. Pipe random pearls on each tier using a no. 1.5 nozzle.

To assemble Insert the dowels and position the polystyrene block (see page 34). Block the base tier with fresh, wired roses (see page 53). Gently move the 9in cake to the edge of the protective board using a palette knife to loosen the cake and allow you to grasp it from underneath. Set the cake over the base tier and dress the top of the cake with fresh roses.

Fabergé

you will need

6in square cake covered with marzipan and ivory sugar paste

template (see page 152)

greaseproof paper

pen

ruler

scribe

12mm (½in) width ribbon to fix around the base of the cake

100g (3½oz) white royal icing

piping bags

no. 3 and no. 1.5 nozzles

topaz lustre

edible gel

paintbrush

fresh flowers to dress

I was inspired to create this cake after visiting a tiara exhibition held at London's Victoria and Albert Museum. Based on an original Fabergé tiara, this traditional-looking cake will suit the most formal of occasions. The design lends itself to a round or square cake as it is repeated four times around each tier. Piping it in white creates an alabaster feel while elements of the pearls are glazed so the cake shimmers.

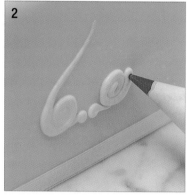

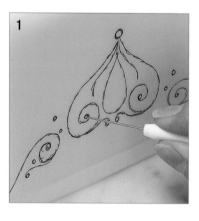

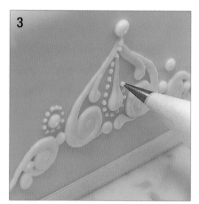

1 Trace the template onto grease-proof paper. Hold the template centrally against the side of the cake (use a ruler to measure the centre accurately and line the top pearl with this mark) and use a scribe to prick the design through. Fix the ribbon around the base tier, securing it with royal icing at the back.

2 Fill 2 separate piping bags with a no. 3 and no. 1.5 nozzle and white royal icing. Using the no. 3 nozzle, pipe the main design, including all the large pearls and pearl drop.

3 Surround the central pearl drop and 2 outer pearls with tiny pearls using the no. 1.5 nozzle as shown. Repeat on all 4 sides and allow to dry.

4 Blend ½ teaspoon of topaz lustre with 1 teaspoon of edible gel and glaze each of the large pearls using a paintbrush as shown. Allow the icing to dry, then dress the top of the cake with fresh flowers.

4-tier Wedgewood-blue Fabergé

This impressive 4-tier round cake has been covered with Wedgewood-blue sugar paste, with the Fabergé design piped in white. For a round cake you will need to measure the circumference accurately using ribbon (see instructions on page 152). I have placed each tier on a board 3in larger than the cake, then blocked the tiers with purple roses and offset each tier.

vanity fair

you will need

3-tier cake covered with marzipan and pink sugar paste placed on boards 3in larger than each tier, covered with pink sugar paste

baseboard 6in larger than the base tier, covered with pink sugar paste

3 boards the same size as the cakes

scribe

royal icing

piping bags and no. 1.5 and no. 3 nozzles

template (see page 154), optional

paintbrush

clear piping gel or topaz lustre mixed with alcohol dipping solution

15mm (⅝in) width ribbon for cakes

25mm (1in) width ribbon for boards

glue stick

grid template (see page 146)

6 dowels

six 9cm (3½in) pillars

pen

ruler

sharp heavy-duty scissors or a junior hacksaw

This design is relatively simple to achieve, yet the end result is effective and elegant. The pearls are hand piped around the top edge of the cake and a simple wide ribbon wrapped around the base. The design works particularly well with contrasting colours and equally well with different-shaped cakes.

1 Position a cake board the same size as each cake carefully on each cake top and scribe around each. Lift the boards off and gently brush away any excess icing. Using a no. 3 nozzle, pipe a single row of large pearls directly over the scribed template marked on the top of each cake. Following the picture, or using the template on page 154, create hanging strands of pearls. Use a no. 1.5 nozzle for the smaller pearls and a no. 3 nozzle for the larger ones. Once the icing is dry, the pearls can be brushed with a glaze – use either clear piping gel or topaz lustre mixed with alcohol dipping solution.

To assemble Fix lengths of the narrower ribbon around each tier and the wider ribbon around the boards. Assemble the tiers following the instructions given on page 36.

4-tier taupe vanity fair

In addition to the pearls around the top lip of each tier, I have included tiny random pearls, piped with a no. 1.5 nozzle, to the sides of this cake. Resplendent and rather regal, this 4-tier stacked cake is beautifully accompanied by the rich, warm colours of silk anemones. Stack the cake (see page 35) after you have decorated and lustred each tier.

art deco

I have had the honoured experience of working with the most prestigious hotels and venues in London. One of my favourite hotels is Claridge's and its architecture, furnishings and colours provided the inspiration for this Art Deco-style cake. Although this is a very stylish design, every panel is a labour of love – allow at least 10 hours to make all 36 panels required (plus a few spares) for this cake.

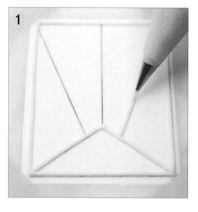

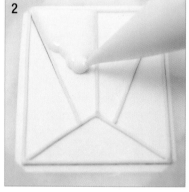

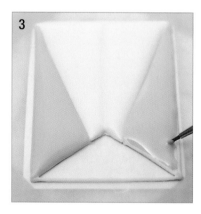

size of square cake	number of panels required
4in	2 each side, 8 total
6in	3 each side, 12 total
8in	4 each side, 16 total
10in	5 each side, 20 total
12in	6 each side, 24 total
14in	7 each side, 28 total
16in	8 each side, 32 total

The template for this cake works for cakes baked in even sizes, but does not lend itself to cakes baked in odd sizes (i.e.7in/9in/11in, etc.).

Tip On the top and bottom tiers, which have an even number of panels, arrange the first side quickly and line up into position by gently sliding the panels. On the middle tier, position the central panel first and work outwards.

1 Begin with all cakes covered and positioned on the iced boards. To make the royal-iced Art Deco panels, place photocopies of the template on page 153 onto a clean work surface that can be left undisturbed overnight and fix into position with masking tape. Place sheets of waxed paper over the top (shiny side up) and fix with masking tape. Using a piping bag fitted with a no. 1.5 nozzle and filled with royal icing, pipe the outline of each panel, ensuring the lines are straight and even.

2 Thin the remainder of the royal icing down with fresh egg white to a runnier consistency as the flooding icing (see page 28). Separate this into 3 equal parts. Colour one third mint green and another light grey. Fill a piping bag with the white flooding icing and snip the very end of the bag with sharp scissors. Flood all the left-hand centre section using a paintbrush to pull and push the icing neatly into the corners. By the time

you have repeated the above for all panels, the icing should have formed enough of a skin to allow you to flood the right-hand centre section. Repeat for all panels.

3 Fill another piping bag with the mint-green icing and flood both side wings on each panel. Because they are not directly touching each other it is fine to flood both before moving on to the next panel.

4 Fill a third piping bag with the grey icing and flood all the base triangles. Allow to dry overnight. Brush the base triangles with silver lustre mixed with alcohol dipping solution. I have found it more effective to quickly apply 2 thin coats rather than brush a single thick coat. These panels can be made in advance and carefully stored in a cake box layered with paper towels. Be careful though as the silver dust rubs off very easily once the alcohol has evaporated.

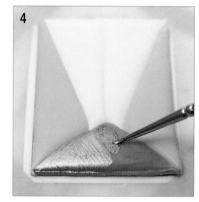

To assemble Peel the panels from the waxed paper using a small cranked palette knife. Pipe a small amount of icing onto the back of each panel and place into position on the cake. Use a ruler to scribe a double line around the board of each tier. Using a no. 1.5 nozzle, pipe grey royal icing over the 2 scribed lines and add evenly spaced curved 'C's all facing the same way. Allow to dry before brushing with silver lustre dissolved in alcohol dipping solution. Edge boards with ribbon and tier the cake as shown on page 36.

strawberry helter-skelter

you will need

10in cake covered with white chocolate plastique

13in and 16in boards covered with white chocolate plastique

500g (1lb 2oz) tempered white chocolate, melted

5 dowels

heavy-duty scissors or a junior hacksaw

8in round board

20cm (8in) diameter x 30cm (12in) high polystyrene cone

paintbrush

1.5kg (3¼lb) white chocolate plastique

rolling pin

icing sugar

1.15kg (2½lb) strawberries

tempered white chocolate for dipping

waxed paper

15mm (⅝in) width cream grosgrain ribbon to edge boards

Tip This cake looks equally impressive when made with dark chocolate plastique and dressed with a mix of soft fruits and berries. See the picture on page 2.

This white chocolate helter-skelter makes a fantastic centrepiece for a very special occasion. Because I have used a polystyrene cone placed on top of a real cake, the finished helter-skelter can be scaled up for even more dramatic effect – I once made one 1.5m (5ft) high! This impressive cake is ideal for large social gatherings, but you will need to have enough extra cutting cake for all your guests, beautifully plated and ready to serve, in the kitchen.

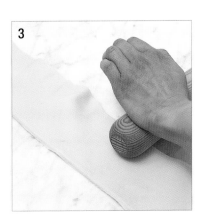

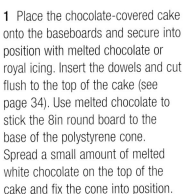

1 Place the chocolate-covered cake onto the baseboards and secure into position with melted chocolate or royal icing. Insert the dowels and cut flush to the top of the cake (see page 34). Use melted chocolate to stick the 8in round board to the base of the polystyrene cone. Spread a small amount of melted white chocolate on the top of the cake and fix the cone into position.

2 Paint the sides of the cake and the entire cone with melted white chocolate. Work quickly as the chocolate plastique will need to be wrapped around before the chocolate sets.

3 Knead the white chocolate plastique until smooth and pliable. Divide into 3 and roll out 2 of the pieces on a work surface lightly dusted with icing sugar into 2 long strips, each approximately 60 x 15cm (24 x 6in). Use a sharp knife to neaten the long edges. Feather one long edge of each strip by pressing down on it with a rolling pin using the ball of your palm.

4 Beginning at the bottom of the cone and with the straight edge of the chocolate strip flush with the base of the cake, carefully wrap the chocolate around the cake and cone as shown. Repeat with the next strip, creating interesting pockets and shapes as you work upwards and finishing with a flourish. Use the final third of white chocolate plastique to make the fans (see page 76). Fix these into position around the cake with melted white chocolate.

To assemble As long as there is no fresh fruit inside the cake it can remain in this state, stored in a cool dry place (but not refrigerated) for up to 3 days. When you are ready to dress the cake, dip strawberries in tempered white chocolate and allow them to cool and harden on waxed paper. Wrap the ribbon around the baseboards, then arrange the dipped strawberries in the pockets formed around the helter-skelter, adding a few around the baseboard.

black-pearl tiara

you will need

8in round cake covered with marzipan
and ivory sugar paste

pen

template (see page 154)

greaseproof paper

masking tape

scribe

piping bags

no. 3, no. 2 and no. 1.5 nozzles

100g (3½oz) black royal icing

12mm (½in) width ribbon to fix around
the base of the cake

fresh flowers and candles to decorate

It is the current fashion for brides to wear beautiful gilded tiaras either with or to replace a lace veil. On this cake, which was inspired by a pearl tiara, I have repeated the pattern around the tier, hand piping pearls of different sizes. This design lends itself to stark contrasting colours, such as black on ivory as used here, or ivory on caramel used on the three-tier cake below. For a truly romantic wedding cake, brush ivory pearls with topaz lustre.

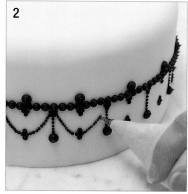

1 Trace the template onto a length of greaseproof paper large enough to fit around the cake (use ribbon to measure). Fix the greaseproof paper around the cake with masking tape and use a scribe to prick the design onto the cake.

2 Fill 3 separate piping bags with a no. 3, no. 2 and no. 1.5 nozzle and black royal icing. Using the no. 3 nozzle, pipe the single row of pearls around the cake, followed by the single large pearls at intervals at the top and bottom. Use the no. 2 nozzle to pipe the diamanté designs and the no. 1.5 nozzle for all the tiny pearls. Allow to dry then fix ribbon around the base of the cake and dress the top with fresh flowers and candles.

3-tier caramel tiara

This sophisticated combination of caramel icing with ivory pearls is one option to complement the current trend for taupe or caramel colours in bridal wear. It also works very well with strong flower colours, such as deep reds, purples and pinks. The colour is achieved by adding caramel or ivory colour to the sugar paste at the kneading stage until the desired intensity is achieved. Make sure you mix sufficient icing at one time as exact colour matches are hard to achieve, and cover the cakes and boards on the same day as the colour will fade over time. For these ivory pearls, mix a little topaz lustre with dipping alcohol solution to create a thin paste and brush it over the pearls with a paintbrush.

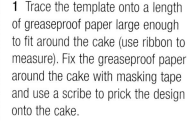
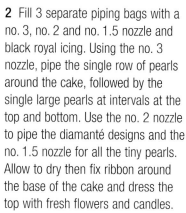

individual cakes

Most of my designs can be transposed onto individual round or square cakes. Other shapes are feasible but trickier to handle. Individual cakes are becoming more fashionable as each guest has his or her own perfectly presented miniature cake, and they are suitable for a variety of occasions. If you are planning a more intimate wedding, include a larger top-tier cake so you can perform the cutting ceremony. (Refer to the guide on page 32 for planning numbers and size of tiers.)

Tip Individual square cakes give you less wastage than round cakes, which are stamped out of a large square cake. If the cakes are to be filled with buttercream, sandwich the large 2 halves together before cutting out the individual cakes.

bumble bees

These are a firm favourite – cute bumble bees with a green-and-white polka-dot ribbon. This cake would be suitable for a child's birthday or christening. Have boxes ready for the guests to take their cake home at the end of the party.

Make the bumble bees' bodies from an elongated ball of yellow paste. Roll the black paste out very thinly and cut narrow black strips and fix these in position over the bumble bees' bodies. Roll out the white petal paste and use a single rose petal cutter to make the wings. Fix these into position with sugar glue. Use a marking tool for the mouth and pipe 2 black eyes. Fix a bumble bee on each individual cake and secure a length of ribbon around each one. Assemble cakes on the stand.

you will need

25 individual round cakes covered with marzipan and sugar paste

3-tier stand – 10in/12in/14in hexagonal tiers covered with sugar paste

yellow, black and white petal paste

1.5cm (½in) rose cutter for the wings

sugar glue

marking tools

100g (3½oz) royal icing

black food coloring

piping bags

no 1.5 nozzle

3m (10ft) length of 15mm (⅝in) width green polka-dot ribbon

numbers

Coloured sugar paste, which I have also used to cover the stand, works well on these individual cakes. The board has been edged in the same ribbon as I have used around the cakes. This cake is a nice idea for a milestone birthday.

Surround each iced cake with a length of ribbon, securing it in position at the back with royal icing. Hand pipe a number on the top of each cake with black royal icing using a piping bag fitted with a no. 3 nozzle. Attach ribbon around each tier of the stand and arrange individual iced cakes around it.

you will need

25 individual round cakes covered with marzipan and red sugar paste

3-tier stand – 8in/11in/14in round tiers covered with red sugar paste

5m (16½ft) length of 15mm (⅝in) width coloured ribbon

100g (3½oz) royal icing

black food colouring

piping bags

no. 3 nozzle

summer garden

you will need

25 individual round cakes covered with marzipan and white sugar paste

6in round cake covered with marzipan and white sugar paste

4-tier hexagonal stand – 8in/10in/12in/14in tiers covered with white sugar paste

5m (16½ft) x 15mm (⅝in) width white ribbon

2m (6½ft) x 6mm (¼in) width lilac ribbon

200g (7oz) royal icing

piping bags and no. 1.5, 2 and 3 nozzles

paintbrushes

cocktail stick

sponge, cut into small pieces

ball tool and foam pad

waxed paper

10g (⅓oz) cocoa butter

food colour dust

100g (3½oz) petal paste

lilac and green food colours

3cm (1¼in) rose cutter

3cm (1¼in) calyx cutter

sugar glue

fresh flowers to dress

These individual cakes feature various decorations and techniques covered in this book – ribbon loops, sugar rose buds, hand-painted flowers and royal-iced butterflies – and I have added a larger full tiffany pearl cake (see page 45) on the top. This is a lovely idea for a more intimate wedding as the bride and groom have a cake for the cutting ceremony.

Decorate 5 mini cakes with white and lilac ribbon loops (see page 49), 5 with sugar butterflies (see page 125), 5 with hand-painted pansies (using the template on page 150 and instructions on page 56), 5 with white rose buds and 5 with lilac rose buds (see page 87). Surround each cake with a length of the wider ribbon overlaid with narrow ribbon, fixing at the back with royal icing. For the top tier, pipe a full tiffany pearl design on the cake as shown using a no. 2 nozzle and white royal icing. Arrange the individual cakes on the lower 3 tiers of the stand and the full tiffany pearl cake on the top tier. Dress the top of the cake with flowers.

Tip I have specified a no. 4 nozzle as the aperture is sufficiently large for a small paintbrush to be inserted to release the polka dot. The petal paste dries and sets very quickly so fix the polka dots onto the cakes as you make them.

polka dots

you will need

25 individual square cakes covered with marzipan and white sugar paste

3-tier stand – 8in/11in/14in round tiers covered with white sugar paste

3m (10ft) length of 15mm (⅝in) width blue ribbon

royal icing

rolling pin

55g (2oz) dusky pink petal paste

55g (2oz) powder blue petal paste

55g (2oz) aqua green petal paste

no. 4 nozzle

thin paintbrush

sugar glue

Decorate your individual cakes with large colourful polka dots for a fun design. Change the colours to complement your theme or use different shapes, such as stars for a Christmas theme or confetti shapes for a wedding.

Surround each iced cake with a length of ribbon secured in position with royal icing. Roll out the petal paste and use the base of a no. 4 plain nozzle to cut out polka dots. Push the end of a small paintbrush through the nozzle to release the polka dot and fix into position on the cake with sugar glue. Arrange the individual cakes on the stand.

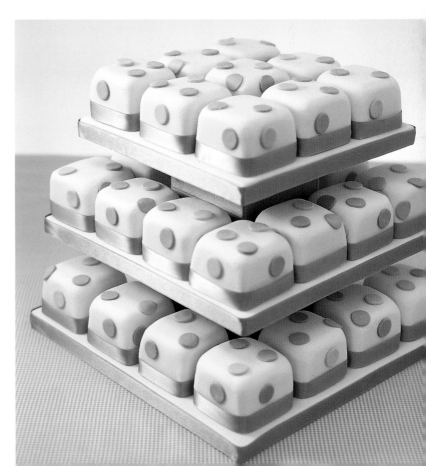

cake templates

MARKING PILLARS ON A CAKE

see pages 36–7

For round and square cakes up to 10in use 4 pillars, positioned at A or B. For larger cakes use 8 pillars, positioned at A and B. For hexagonal and heart-shaped tiers use either 3 or 6 pillars, positioned at C, D or a combination of both.

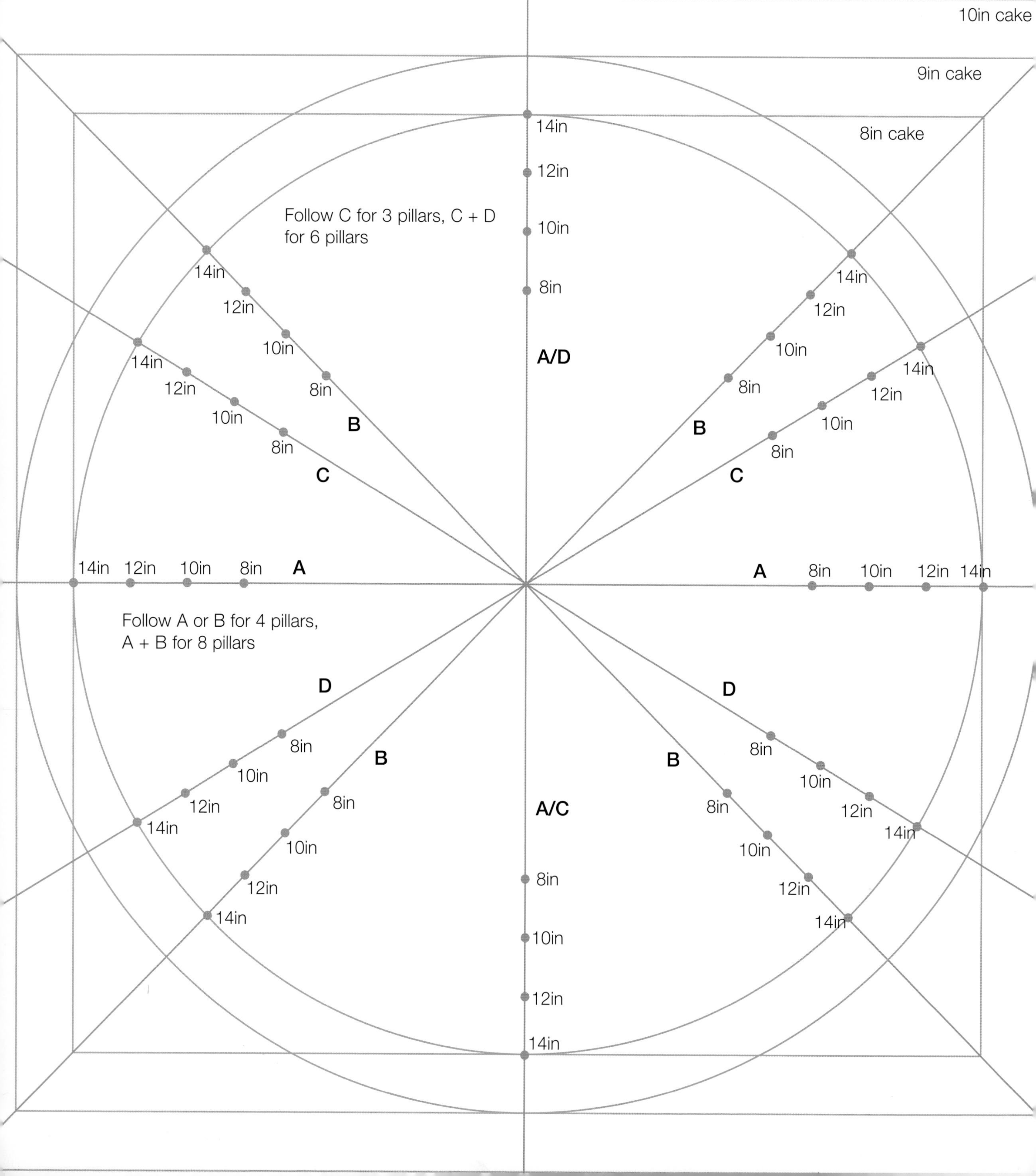
10in cake
9in cake
8in cake
14in
12in
10in
8in
A/D
Follow C for 3 pillars, C + D for 6 pillars
14in
12in
10in
8in
B
14in
12in
10in
8in
C
14in
12in
10in
8in
B
14in
12in
10in
8in
C
14in 12in 10in 8in A
A 8in 10in 12in 14in
Follow A or B for 4 pillars, A + B for 8 pillars
D
8in
10in
12in
14in
B
8in
10in
12in
14in
A/C
8in
10in
12in
14in
D
8in
10in
12in
14in
B
8in
10in
12in
14in

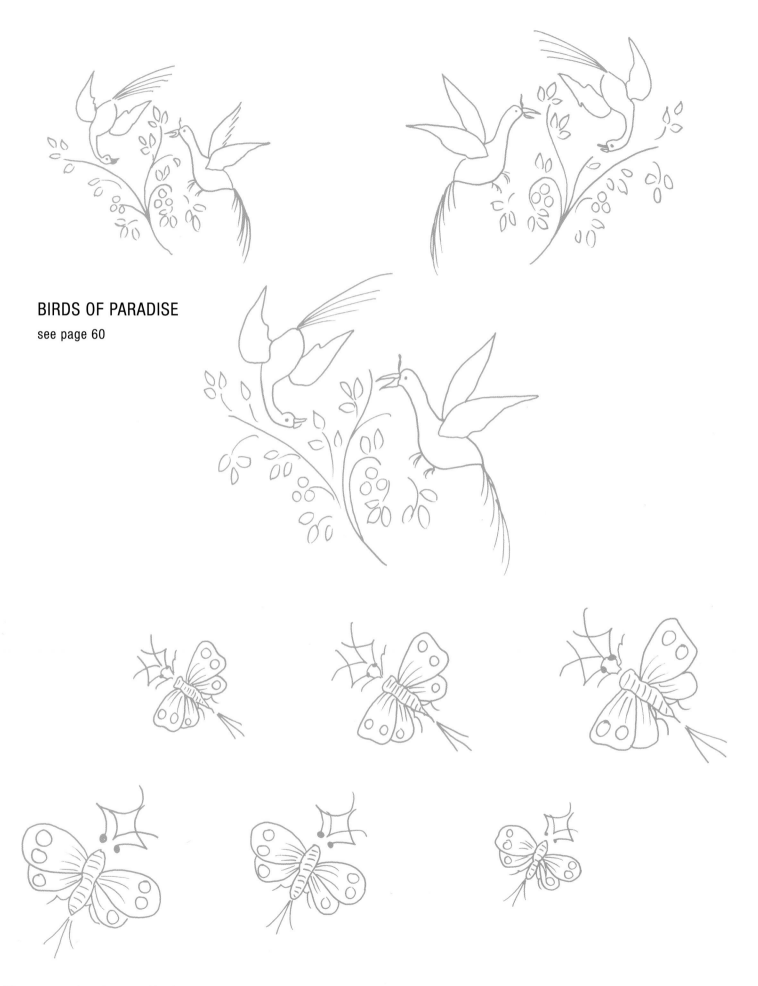

BIRDS OF PARADISE

see page 60

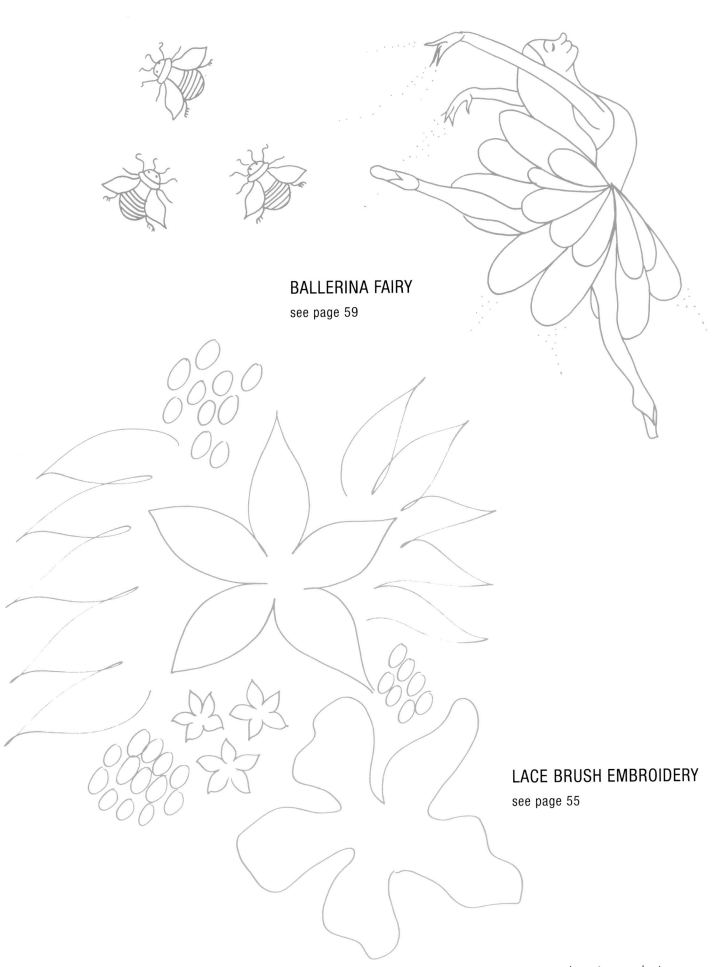

BALLERINA FAIRY

see page 59

LACE BRUSH EMBROIDERY

see page 55

INDIVIDUAL CHRISTMAS

see page 102

BIRTHDAY CLOWN

see page 110

INDIVIDUAL PANSY

see page 143

FLOODED BUTTERFLIES

see page 125

FLEUR-DE-LIS

see page 126

I have found the following to be the most accurate way to ensure that the design lines up perfectly on each tier. Measure the circumference of the tier accurately using ribbon and divide this circumference into 6. Adapt the given template so it fits exactly by stretching or condensing the scrolls slightly. Align the base of a long sheet of greaseproof paper against the base of the template. Using a waterproof black fibretip pen (pencil will mark the cake), trace the first sixth of the template. Flip the greaseproof paper over and line up to draw the next sixth. This will provide one symmetrical copy of the design. Repeat until the design has been drawn a total of 6 times to provide 3 full symmetrical copies of the design.

FABERGÉ 4-TIER

see page 130

For a round cake you will need to measure the circumference accurately using ribbon. Divide the ribbon into 4 by folding it in half then in half again. Starting at the back and base of the cake, mark both ends of a quarter length of ribbon, then move it around the cake until all 4 quarters are accurately marked. Position the template centrally between 2 of the points and scribe. Repeat for the whole tier.

SECOND TIER

THIRD TIER

BASE TIER

TOP TIER

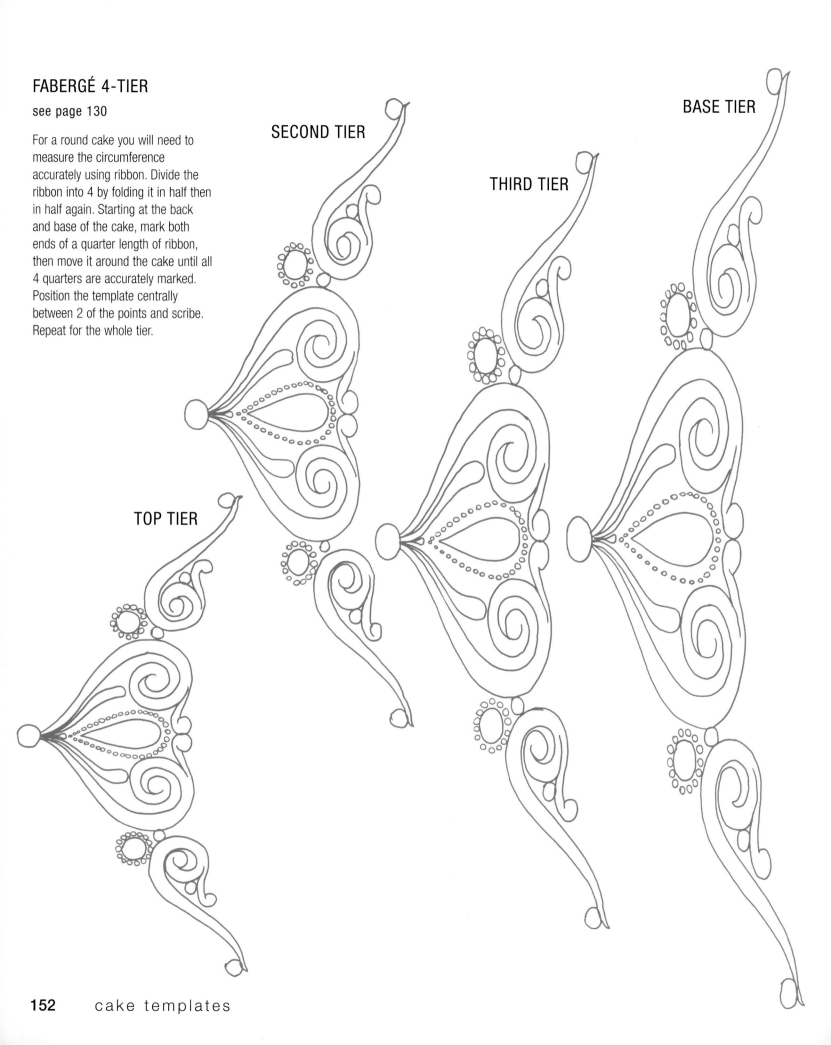

ART DECO

see page 134

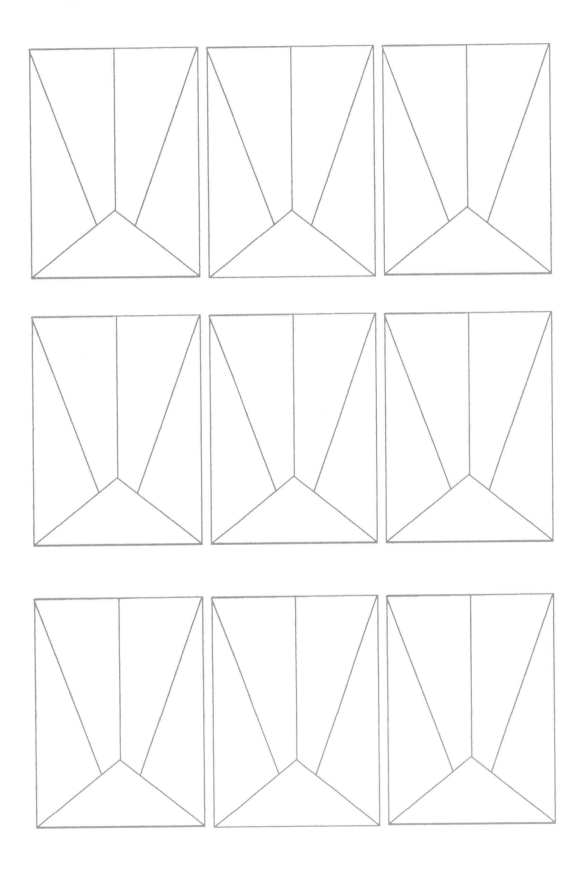

CATLIA LACE
see page 52

BLACK-PEARL TIARA
see page 138

VANITY FAIR
see page 133

BUILDING BLOCKS, TEDDY BEAR CHRISTENING, INDIVIDUAL NUMBERS
see pages 109, 112 and 140

ABCDEFGHIJKLM
NOPQRSTUVWXYZ

abcdefghijklmnopqrstuvwxyz

ABCDEFGHIJKLM
NOPQRSTUVWXYZ

1234567890
1234567890

useful addresses

cake decorating supplies

Continental Chef Supplies
The Courtyard
South Hetton Industrial Estate
South Hetton
County Durham
DH6 2UZ
Tel 0808 100 1777
www.chefs.net

Divertimenti
Tel 0870 129 5027
www.divertimenti.co.uk

Lakeland
www.lakelandlimited.com

Little Venice Cake Company
15 Manchester Mews
Marylebone
London W1U 2DX
Tel 020 7486 5252
www.LVCC.co.uk

Squires Shop
Squires House
3 Waverley Lane
Farnham
Surrey
GU9 8BB
Tel 0845 225 5671
www.squires-shop.com

Sugar Shack
87 Burntoak Broadway
Burntoak
Middlesex
HA8 5EP
Tel 0800 597 5097
www.sugarshack.co.uk

Surbiton Art and Sugarcraft
140 Hook Road
Surbiton
Surrey
KT6 5BZ
Tel: 020 8391 4664
www.surbitonart.co.uk

florists

Neil Birks
5 Grosvenor Cottages
Eaton Terrace
London SW1W 8HA
Tel 020 7259 9746 / 07770 881323
Email: neil@nbflowers.co.uk
www.nbflowers.co.uk

Rob Van Helden Floral Design Ltd.
8 Tun Yard
Peardon Street
London SW8 3HT
Tel 020 7720 6774
www.rvhfloraldesign.com

Simon Lycett
30 Charter House Works
Eltringham Street
London SW18 1TD
Tel 020 8874 1040
Email: enquiries@simonlycett.co.uk
www.simonlycett.co.uk

Paula Pryke
The Flower House
Cynthia Street
London N1 9JF
Tel 020 7837 7336
ww.paula-pryke-flowers.com

Paul Thomas
The Greenery
4 Shepherd Street
London W1J 7JD
Tel 020 7499 6889
www.paulthomasflowers.co.uk

ribbons

Narrow Fabric Company
Waylands, Pound Lane
Nailsea
Bristol
BS48 2AT
Tel 01275 859585/810766
www.narrowfabric.co.uk

VV Rouleaux
6 Marylebone High Street
London W1U 4NJ
Tel 020 7224 5179
and
54 Sloane Square
London SW1W 8AX
Tel 020 7730 3125
www.vvrouleaux.com

wedding planners

Siobhan Craven-Robins
70 Gun Place
86 Wapping Lane
London E1W 2RX
Tel 020 7481 4338

Deborah Dwek Weddings
Deborah Dwek Limited
9 Hayward Road
London N20 0HA
Tel 020 8446 9501 / 07941 660763
Email debbie.dwek@lineone.net
www.deborahdwekweddings.co.uk

Kathryn Lloyd Wedding Design
152 Grosvenor Road
London SW1V 3JL
Tel / Fax 020 7828 5535
www.kathrynlloyd.co.uk

Orchid Events
Suite16
45 Marlborough Place
London NW8 0PX
Tel 020 7625 2122
www.orchidevents.co.uk

event planners

The Admirable Crichton
Unit 5 Camberwell Trading Estate
Denmark Road
London SE5 9LB
Tel 020 7326 3800
www.admirable-crichton.co.uk

Bentley's Entertainments
7 Square Rigger Row
Plantation Wharf
London SW11 3TZ
Tel 020 7223 7900

Party Planners
56 Ladbroke Grove
London W11 2PB
Tel 020 7229 9666

index

acknowledgements

I have heard it said that 'everyone has a book in them' and for me that book has always been about cakes! To see a collection of my spectacular cakes published is truly 'the icing on the cake'. It has been made possible with a little help from my friends:

Firstly, I would like to thank my amazing team – past and present – at Little Venice Cake Company: Andrea Markham for flapping your cuffs and assisting with the chocolate cakes; Bee Davies for bringing the character designs to life in sugar; Christine Lee for preparing the sugar flowers; Julie Anne Deane, 'back down under' with Clint and Baba; Amanda Sherlock and Rosie Crichton for keeping me on the straight and narrow.

I am humbled to work with such a talented publishing team: a huge thank you to Jacqui Small for giving me the wonderful opportunity to indulge in my passion and to Kate John for orchestrating this entire project. Thank you Maggie Town for your most expert and discerning eye for design and layout – I love it; thank you Anne McDowall for decrypting and editing my text and learning the names of the cakes; and a special thank you to Janine Hosegood for your outstanding photography. Thank you all for ploughing through so many cakes!

I am honoured and privileged to work in an industry with so many talented event organizers, party planners, banqueting teams, caterers and florists. The support and belief of so many has helped to propel LVCC to become the prestigious company it is today. I would particularly like to thank Neil Birks, Rob Van Helden and Paul Thomas for your most beautiful flowers and James Partridge for allowing me to adopt Claridge's as my home from home.

A very heartfelt thank you to my family: my parents Ralph and Celia for being there, always, and to Greg and Tanti Max, to whom I dedicate the bumble bees.

Finally, I am hugely grateful to Marie-Louise Sessions (née Wilson), my A-level lecturer, for asking me to decorate her wedding cake when I was 17. Thank you for your belief in me, and the incentive that gave me to discover my career.